EARLY PRAISE

"*THE CLOAK* IS A VERY HONEST AND READABLE MEMOIR. THERE ARE THE CHALLENGES, STRUGGLES AND JOYS OF SUCCESSIVE RELATIONSHIPS, THEIR BEGINNINGS AND ENDINGS, AND A CONSTANT QUEST FOR MEANING IN AND THROUGH THOSE RELATIONSHIPS. THE ACCOUNTS FROM 'LIVED EXPERIENCE' AS AN ANALYSAND IN JUNGIAN ANALYSIS, AND AS A PSYCHOTHERAPIST, WERE A REVELATION TO ME. I HAVE NEVER QUITE UNDERSTOOD BEFORE WHAT 'INDIVIDUATION' MEANS—NOW I KNOW."

- **Michael Wright,** Emeritus Professor, Psychology and Cognitive Neuroscience, Brunel University, Uxbridge

"AN HONEST AND FASCINATING ACCOUNT OF THE AUTHOR'S STRUGGLE TO GET FREE OF THE POWER GAMES IN RELATION TO HER MOTHER, HER MARRIAGE, HER LOVER AND THE PSYCHOANALYTIC ORGANISATION THAT SHOULD HAVE BEEN ABLE TO HELP HER FIND HERSELF."

- **Professor Michael Jacobs,** PhD, author of *The Presenting Past*

"AT TIMES, HEARTBREAKING. AT OTHER TIMES EXHILARATING, AND THOUGHT-PROVOKING...A FASCINATING BOOK, AND I REALLY ENJOYED EVERY PAGE OF IT."

- **Stephan Roman,** historian and author of *Isle and Empires*

"VIRGINIA HOPES HER BOOK WILL INSPIRE THOSE WHO ARE DRAWN TO ENGAGE CONSCIOUSLY IN THEIR INDIVIDUATION PROCESS. I THINK IT WILL. CERTAINLY, SHE WILL HELP OTHERS TO TRY TO BE HONEST. AND SHE WILL HELP MANY PEOPLE TO PERCEIVE WHAT A WEALTH OF EXPERIENCES LIE WITHIN THE PSYCHE."

- **Dr Roderick Peters,** LRCP, MRCS, MBBS, MRCP

"WHAT AN ASTONISHING WORK, I COULDN'T STOP READING, IT IS FASCINATING FROM START TO FINISH."

- **Dr Graham** Lennox, FRCP, consultant neurologist

"THIS IS A FASCINATING BOOK. HONEST, BRAVE, INSIGHTFUL. VIRGINIA ROUTH LYNCH IS PASSIONATE ABOUT CARL JUNG AND INTRODUCES SOME OF HIS CONCEPTS ELEGANTLY AND INSIGHTFULLY, MAKING IT A WONDERFUL INTRODUCTION TO ANYONE INTERESTED IN EXPLORING DREAMS AND VENTURING ON A JOURNEY OF SELF-DISCOVERY."

- **Lucinda Montefiore,** radio producer

THE CLOAK

an inspirational account of personal transformation

VIRGINIA ROUTH LYNCH

The Cloak: An Inspirational Account of Personal Transformation
Copyright © 2022 Virginia Routh Lynch

This book is a work of memoir. Everything in this account is true and reflects the author's recollections of experiences over time, as remembered at the time it was written and verified by referential accounts from the author's own diaries and journals from the time period covered in the work. Occasionally, dialogue consistent with the character or nature of the person speaking has been supplemented or recreated, and some events have been compressed. All persons within are actual individuals; there are no composite characters. Concerning those public figures mentioned in this book, the writing is based on the author's memory of these people and the interactions they had with one another. These individuals may have remembered their impact on the author differently. All poems courtesy of the Virginia Routh Lynch. Excerpts from the *I Ching* reprinted based on author's own paraphrasing from original journal entries, referencing the open source English translation from Chinese by James Legge, *The Yî King* (1882), as published in *Sacred Books of the East, vol. XVI. 2nd edition* (1899).

Publisher's Cataloguing-in-Publication data

Names: Lynch, Virginia Routh, author.
Title: The Cloak : an account of individuation based on diaries and journals / Virginia Routh Lynch.
Description: Seattle, WA: All She Wrote Productions, 2022.
Identifiers: LCCN: 2022914168 | ISBN: 9780996899369 (hardcover) | 9780996899390 (paperback) | 9781958564899 (ebook) | 9781958564998 (audio) | 9781958564981 (library)
Subjects: LCSH Lynch, Virgina Routh. | Psychologists–Biography. | Jungian psychology. | Individuation (Psychology) | Psychoanalytic interpretation–Case studies. | BISAC BIOGRAPHY & AUTOBIOGRAPHY / Personal Memoirs | BIOGRAPHY & AUTOBIOGRAPHY / Social Scientists & Psychologists | PSYCHOLOGY / Movements / Jungian
Classification: LCC BF175 .L96 2022 | DDC 150.19/54092–dc23

Library of Congress Control Number: 2022914168

Hardcover: 9780996899369
Paperback: 9780996899390
Ebook: 9781958564899
Audiobook (retail): 9781958564998
Audiobook (library): 9781958564981

Cover Design by Thea Chard
Book Design by All She Wrote Productions

All She Wrote Productions
www.allshewroteproductions.com

Seattle, WA | USA

CONTENTS

THE CLOAK

INTRODUCTION

by Dr Roderick Peters LRCP, MRCS, MBBS, MRCP

Member of International Association of Jungian Analysts and training analyst for Society for Analytical Psychology, British Confederation of Psychotherapists, and Westminster Pastoral Foundation and Guild of Analytical Psychology

VIRGINIA'S BOOK DOES not need another introduction because she introduces it herself and explains her use of terms which might be unfamiliar to some readers.

What I will contribute, then, are some perspectives on the phenomenon in human life that Jung called 'Individuation', and how Virginia's book describes her experience of it.

Briefly, individuation is the way in which the 'I', the ego, ever more completely represents the Self, from which it was born. The ego is the centre of the field of conscious psyche. The Self is the centre of being in its entirety, conscious and unconscious psyche, spirit and matter.

Many people uneducated in psychology often speak of ego as a bad thing, meaning too much boastfulness, entitlement, greed, and self-importance. But the ego is a very, *very* important structure in the psyche. It begins to grow, to take shape, in earliest infancy. Many powerful influences act upon its development. Experiences of approvals and disapprovals, fears and ambitions, love or disregard, come firstly from mother figures, then the nuclear family, the extended family, the neighbourhood society, schools and further education, religious institutions, and national and international society—ever widening circles of collective psyche, conscious and unconscious.

These relentless influences lead to parts of oneself being repressed, hidden, denied, etc., and other parts being magnified, proudly thrust into the light.

If my mind and body are like a car, then my ego has to be, and tries very hard to be, the competent driver. The ego is the CEO for the management of most social life, and it has to be a well built and strong entity to manage modern civilised life. If it is too weak a person will not be able to manage complex human life (like the woman patient described in Virginia's account). If it is too open to the unconscious psyche it will be alternately inflated and deflated by archetypal identifications. If it is too open to the collective consciousness it will simply identify with attitudes and beliefs prevailing in the group or the media, and severely limit a person's acquaintance with their own self.

So, to return to my initial statement, individuation connotes how the ego ever more completely represents the Self in consciousness.

Individuation is a normal process. It happens to everyone as they get older. It is, as it were, a side effect of the mortal state of limitation in time and space. But if the ego and conscious psyche direct attention to the process, and channel energy into it, it will proceed faster and become deeper.

Probably the single most important change that can come about in the process of individuation is when the ego truly kneels before the Self, and truly knows, more or less for the first time, that it is only a proponent of that Self for the purposes of a life in time and space. It sees that it is not the King or Queen; it is the representative of that majesty.

When the ego recognises Self as the true centre, it does not become weaker, it becomes stronger.

Knowing, accepting, integrating all the parts of human nature that one has hidden, denied, repressed, suppressed, or never known at all, does not mean that the ego then acts them out. Quite the reverse—so long as one does not know these shadowy qualities are part of one, they will sometimes have been acted out without conscious scrutiny, causing all sorts of problems. But when one knows them, one can choose when and whether to use them.

Virginia's account of a period of her life is quite naked. She expresses herself with a degree of honesty that few people can match.

The reader is introduced to a rather wild person, passionate, turbulent, intensely conflicted, experiencing recurrent swings between opposites such as admiration and contempt, self love and self hatred, doubt and certainty, power and weakness.

It seems that—perhaps by nature, or perhaps as a result of the wounding from a star-crossed mother relationship—Virginia has always felt close to, aware of, the archetypal realm.

During most of the first half of her life she exerted herself passionately, trying to make real the ideals and perfect states of the archetypal realm in the mortal world. The impossibility of achieving this caused states of uncomfortable make-believe for long periods of time. And having such a strong sense of the sacred, the numinous, the holy, within her, she was contemptuous and dismissive of the compromised institutions which claim to mediate God to mortals.

This book, The Cloak, tells us how she lived through these times, these stages of individuation, and how she came to realise the true relationship of her ego to the archetypes, and the central archetype—the Self—was to be found with the living psyche. Pursuing this seems to have brought peace and tranquillity.

Relationships with her family of origin, her husbands and other lovers, her children, her teachers, her therapists, her professional colleagues, and her patients, are conveyed with sharp aliveness. We, the readers, go with her along her white water river, and see how she increasingly turns toward her Self, using self scrutiny, diaries, dreams, visions, and active imagination to masticate, digest and assimilate the life she's experiencing. 'The Cloak', her book title, comes from an especially meaningful active imagination.

Virginia hopes her book will inspire those who are drawn to engage consciously in their individuation process. I think it will. Certainly, she will help others to try to be honest. And she will help many people to perceive what a wealth of experiences lie within the psyche.

– Dr Roderick Peters
Surrey, March 2022

GLOSSARY

MOST OF THE terminology that I use in this book should be self-explanatory from the context in which it is used. Here is a brief survey of the psychological words for those who want a quick point of reference. They are not precise definitions; this is readily available on the internet.

ACTIVE IMAGINATION is a way of accessing the unconscious by writing down fantasies.

ARCHETYPES are images that emerge from the collective unconscious in the form of myths and symbols.

ANIMUS/ANIMA: THE animus is the inner masculine part of a woman. The anima is the inner feminine part of a man. Becoming conscious of these figures is an essential part of individuation.

COLLECTIVE UNCONSCIOUS, as its name suggests, belongs to everybody. It is the substratum of everybody's psyche and is the source of creativity and destructiveness. C.G. Jung's achievement was exploring the collective unconscious and recording what he found.

COMPLEXES are psychological wounds, usually from childhood.

DREAMS can be understood objectively or subjectively. In an objective interpretation, the figures in a dream represent people in the dreamer's life. In a subjective interpretation, the people in a dream represent parts of the dreamer. For instance, a dream about being driven in a car by X could be interpreted two ways: approached objectively, it is interpreted as a comment on the dreamer's relationship with X; approached subjectively, the interpretation would suggest that X is a part of the dreamer. Both viewpoints are usually explored when working on a dream.

EGO: This is how you see yourself and how you operate in the world. It is your history, your thoughts, your ambitions, your body. The first part of individuation does not go any further than this. In itself, this is an achievement—to have a strong ego and know your shadow (*see* Personal Unconscious) means confidence and self-knowledge. But it is only the beginning of the journey.

INDIVIDUATION: An individual's unique psychological journey.

INFLATION: This happens when ego becomes puffed up. It often occurs when ego identifies with an archetype.

NARCISSISM is similar to inflation, but it is not the same. It occurs when ego identifies with the Self and assumes God-like qualities.

NEGATIVE TRANSFERENCE is unconsciously putting onto the therapist the anger and hostility felt towards parents in childhood.

PERSONAL UNCONSCIOUS: Jung uses the term 'shadow' for the personal unconscious. It contains everything within a person's psyche that could be made conscious—things that have been repressed or rejected, such as complexes, but also unacknowledged gifts and potential. The more the ego is able to integrate its shadow, the stronger the ego becomes.

PROJECTION: Unconsciously attributing to others parts of yourself.

PSYCHE comes from the Greek word *psykhe*, meaning all the elements of the human mind.

REPRESSION is the act of suppressing a thought or feeling so that it remains unconscious.

SELF is the divine centre of each person and their potential. Hindus call it Atman, Buddhists call it enlightenment or Nirvana. In Taoism it is called Tao. In Judaism it is called God. In the Upanishads it is the Self. The Christian symbols of the cross, the kingdom of heaven and the holy child are all symbols of the Self.

SHADOW *see* Personal Unconscious.

SYMBOL is anything that stands for or represents something else. For instance, a known object, such as a hat, can symbolise something else that may be abstract, such as status.

SYNCHRONICITY: Meaningful coincidence.

TRANSFERENCE is unconsciously associating the other person with a past relationship.

FOREWORD

FROM 1975 TO 1986, I kept a record of the extraordinary events that were turning my life upside down. I wrote the journals in order to steady myself, to try to make sense of the experiences I was being buffeted by. I kept the record in notebooks, large, small, all colours and sizes. They were not intended for anybody else. I stored them on the top of the bookshelf. During the past forty years, I often looked at the journals and tried to work on them, but something in me seemed blocked, and I would put them back on the bookshelf. In those years I have moved five times. Each time, the notebooks came with me, though one or two may have been lost in the process.

In February 2020, a conversation with a friend stimulated me to go back and look at the notebooks again. We had been to an exhibition of Islamic Art and afterwards this led us to discuss our different passions. Hers had begun with pattern cutting, then geometry leading on to Islamic art. She assumed my passion was music. I realised then, with a jolt, that although music is very important to me, the overwhelming passion of my life is individuation. It is like a substratum running through my life that I rarely talk about. And that afternoon, in the British Museum, it jumped back into consciousness.

When I got home, I took the notebooks down from the shelf where they had been collecting dust and started to read them. I knew immediately that now I was ready to work on them. My first inclination was to produce a transcript of the notebooks without editing or altering anything, and to publish them for other people to read. But I soon realised that the notebooks contained raw material that had to be sifted, explained and interpreted before readers could understand my experiences. Therefore, over the last two years, I have been writing this book based on the material in the journals.

It may seem that this book is about me but that is not my underlying intention. I have written this account to illustrate how the individuation process can transform people's lives. My experience is not a template for how it will be for anybody else. Each journey is individual, each person has to find their own way. For me, dreams and active imaginations led me; for other people it could be meditation, creative arts or nature. Analysis is not a prerequisite for individuation—but, like any new journey, it is easier if you have a guide. The common factor for everybody is the need to listen to their inner voice.

Individuation is a natural process. We see it in nature when an acorn develops into an oak tree or an egg into a chick and then into a hen. With human beings there is the natural process of physical development, but we are also capable of psychological development, and this is what C.G. Jung calls individuation. But unlike physical development, individuation requires an individual to consciously co-operate with the process.

This cannot happen until the ego is firm and secure. If the ego is damaged (the image of a broken vessel I find helpful) it would be further shattered by contact with the unconscious. Therefore, facing childhood trauma and addressing complexes (the wounds from childhood) are the first necessary steps to take, so that the vessel, though flawed, can be mended. This means that childhood wounds have to be addressed. Many people never get beyond this point. Followers of Freudian psychoanalysis rarely go further. They equate the unconscious with personal contents that have been repressed. They ignore the collective unconscious, the substratum that underlies all our lives and belongs to all of us. They believe that conscious functioning is all that matters and shut out from their lives the abundant richness and creativity that lies in the collective unconscious.

Many people are stuck in one dimension; they have developed their conscious functioning, their rational thinking, and are often very successful in their careers. But when they reach middle age, something starts to rattle as they repeat themselves. They find that what worked in the past doesn't work now to make life happy and fulfilling. They start to feel disillusioned and sometimes depressed. "It's just your age," people will tell them. I want to tell them that this is not the time for settling for the mundane life, but rather an opportunity to expand their personality. I want to tell them that their feelings of staleness and futility are the psyche urging them to recognise the limitations of ego consciousness and to find parts of themselves they didn't even know existed. The journey of individuation beckons us all—it urges us to listen to our inner voice and have the courage to obey it.

Jung was not the first person to describe individuation. The alchemists in the Middle Ages wrote copiously about it. The mystics, Hildegard of Bingham and St Teresa of Avila, and modern mystics such as Evelyn Underhill, also describe it. But Jung brought it forward into everyday life by explaining it in psychological terms.

- Dorset, March 2022

CHILDHOOD

I WAS BORN Virginia Raphael in London, England in 1935. For the first five years, I lived in St Mark's Square, Regents Park, with my mother, father, my older sister, Juliet, and my younger brother, Adam. A nanny looked after us and there was also a cook and a housemaid. Both my parents were Jewish. My father, Geoffrey, was a barrister. His family owned an optical factory in Tottenham Court Road where my father worked for many years. He attended evening classes to study law and was called to the bar when he was nearly 40. Shortly after this, he met my mother, Nancy (née Rose). Geoffrey was fourteen years older.

Nancy had studied sociology at the London School of Economics. There she became friends with many Labour politicians such as Hugh Gaitskell and Hugh Dalton. She came from a wealthy Jewish family who considered my father to be socially inferior and opposed their marriage. My father was offended by their attitude and never forgave them.

Loneliness pervaded my childhood. I was always looking for a companion, a best friend. My sister Juliet and I were very close in age and were treated like twins when we were little; we had a twin pram and were dressed alike. I always followed in Juliet's footsteps; she was only thirteen months ahead of me, but she seemed to me bigger and more intelligent than I was. It was clearly infuriating for her to have a younger sister trying to catch her up. She was never supportive or loving to me.

In 1940, we three children went to the United States with Nancy to live in Princeton, New Jersey, for the duration of the war because, like many Jewish families, my parents were frightened of invasion. Juliet was six, I was five and Adam was two. It must have been a huge change of life for Nancy to be in charge of three children with nobody to help her. She adored Juliet and Adam. The way she coped with the awkward second daughter was to ignore her, and so the sick pattern of behaviour began. I discovered the way to be noticed was to show off, throw my weight around, be outrageous. I was annoying, irritating–everything Adam and Juliet were not. This would make Nancy angry. In a strange way, I was rewarded for being naughty. The more awful I was, the more attention I got.

Soon after we arrived in Princeton, I realised that Juliet didn't like me. She spurned me, always preferring friends from school or the neighbourhood, leaving me out of games, making me feel decidedly second best. The problems with my brother Adam compounded it. My mother told me that I was jealous of Adam, and on the face of it that made sense. He was a gorgeous little boy with large blue eyes and very long eyelashes, doted on by my mother and everybody else. But now I think my fury with Adam has a different explanation. Before we left for the States, Nanny, who had looked after us since we were babies, said to me that I must look after Adam, because she wasn't coming with us. And I was keen to do so. But he wasn't very keen to be mothered by me! He pushed me away, which made me feel rejected and furious. So I was isolated in the family. Juliet was the perfect daughter, Adam the perfect son, and me? I was a pain in the neck, either showing off to get attention or in a bad mood because nothing was going my way.

In Princeton, I shared a bedroom with Adam, which I hated because he pestered and teased me. Juliet had her own room. I remember talking to the photo of Geoffrey in army uniform on top of the cupboard in Nancy's bedroom. I thought that when the war was over, everything would be alright again because Daddy would sort it out. When I was mooching around, feeling miserable, if Nancy asked what was wrong, I would say I was missing Daddy. The truth was, I was missing Nanny. But I couldn't say this because I thought it might hurt Nancy's feelings. I longed to have friends like Juliet did, to be popular and chosen as a partner in games at school, and, most important of all, I longed to be loved by my mother. But my mother didn't want me around.

Why did this happen? A large part of my motivation for studying psychology was in order to understand my mother and the strange dynamic between us. My mother, Nancy, was the eldest of four. She and her brother, Jim, were the stars of the family. Socially, they were admired by everybody—they were very attractive and charming; everybody loved their company. Their mother, Dula, was a little woman in stature but huge in ambition for her children. Nancy and Jim were the apples of her eye. For Nancy, her mother's ambition put unbearable pressure on her and she couldn't sustain the golden girl image. The intolerable darkness that she carried within her, caused severe depressions throughout her life. When I was born, thirteen months after Juliet, Nancy became severely depressed and rejected me. But fortunately for me, Nanny was in charge of the nursery and for five years I was looked after with love.

⚜

Bad girl
Casts a cloud
Fat, slobbish
Nobody likes her
And neither do I
It is my fault
I am bad,
If I wasn't so selfish
I wouldn't upset others
If I was nicer
People would like me
If I tried a bit harder
I could be a good girl
It's all my fault
I just need to try harder
Make more effort
Then Mum will love me
Like she loves the others
It is not her fault she doesn't
I don't blame her at all
Who could like an ugly
Uninteresting person
Who can't make jokes
And is always in the way
A nuisance
A pain in the neck

After the war ended, we came back to England on a boat with lots of children who had been separated from their parents. I remember playing with them, building card houses. We were in the dining room, having breakfast, when we docked at Liverpool. Nancy suddenly shouted "Geoff!" and rushed across the room to greet our father who had somehow managed to get onto the boat. When I looked at this tall, dark man walking toward us, I immediately felt huge disappointment. "He looks like Adolf Hitler," I muttered to myself. My heart sank as I realised that he was not the saviour I had hoped he would be. During all those years of misery in the States, I had pinned my hopes on Daddy, that somehow, he would put everything right once he was home. But when I saw him, I realised that he was no hero, and he couldn't sort out my problems.

We went back to live in London at our old house in St Mark's Square. Juliet and I attended the same school, Francis Holland. Juliet was surrounded by friends. I had a few, but in my eyes, they were not a patch on Juliet's friends. There was always this loneliness in me, this longing to find a soulmate, someone I could talk to, who would love me.

My moodiness, bad temper and irritating behaviour were a problem for the family. Nancy decided to send me away to boarding school in the hope that this would sort me out. She chose St Felix, a boarding school in Southwold, Suffolk, because she had been there herself. The headmistress of Francis Holland, Miss Joslin, gave me extra lessons in chemistry to prepare me for St Felix. I was so embarrassed by this that I couldn't concentrate on what she was trying to teach me. I was in a daze of unhappiness most of the time, trying to understand what was wrong with me, why my mother disliked me, why nobody seemed to like me. St Felix seemed like an opportunity to make a fresh start and I looked forward to it. There I would have friends, I reassured myself. There people would like me.

As I stood on the platform waiting for the train to Halesworth at the beginning of my first term, I was humiliated to find that I was the only girl not wearing the camel hair regulation school coat. Mine was the same sort of colour, but tweed with a velvet collar. As I had this coat already, Nancy did not want to spend extra money on a school coat. We didn't have much money at that time, because my grandmother, Dula, held the purse strings to the family money and, as she did not approve of my mother's marriage, she withheld money from her. Therefore, at that time, we were reliant on my father's salary. I remember my mother crying as she did the family accounts because there was not enough money to pay for the household expenses.

Once we were on the train, I met a lively girl called Eve Austin who was also going to be in Somerville, the house I was allocated to. "Oh, do let's be friends!" I said to her, to my lasting shame. Eve teased me mercilessly about saying this.

It was cold and bleak at St Felix. Blistering winds blew in from the North Sea. There was a small coal fire in the study, which we clustered around. I remember chilblains on hands and feet, itchy red things. Miss Williamson, the headmistress, was an austere woman with short white hair. Once a week, we went to her house where she would read books to us. Most of the lessons bored me. There was no teacher who engaged me in learning. I spent most of the time gazing out of the window or watching the clock.

I was always looking for a soulmate, someone I could really talk to and share ideas with. I had two friends at St Felix, but neither were on my wavelength. I was lonely and often bored. We were not allowed to go for walks on our own. Lessons didn't engage me and I never listened to the teachers. I think teaching was probably rather poor because St Felix was in an isolated part of Suffolk and young teachers would not have wanted to work there. I remember a history teacher coming down from London for the day to teach the form above us; she was said to be very interesting. I sat outside the door of the classroom trying, unsuccessfully, to hear what she was saying.

Music was my passion at school. I counted the days to my violin lessons and fell in love with my violin teacher, Ivey Dickson. I used to pick flowers to put in her room each week before she came to the school from London. I led the school orchestra and played solos at most of the school concerts, but usually very badly, as playing in public made me feel acutely nervous.

I was very sad that I was not in the choir, which was the jewel in the crown of music at St Felix. The choir sang on the BBC sometimes, and also at the Proms. Being in the choir meant sitting in the organ gallery during the chapel services and having a hymn book with the four singing parts in it. Each year I auditioned for a place in the choir. The successful applicants' names were posted on a board at the end of the school year. Each year my name was not on the list. In my last year, I asked the head of music why I was not successful.

"Oh, Virginia," she said. "I thought you knew. We don't have Jewish girls in the choir." Strange as it may seem, I was pleased to hear this because it meant there was nothing wrong with my singing voice. Anti-Semitism seemed an established fact. It did not occur to me then that it was wrong. But when I told my mother about this, when I was home for the holidays, she was very angry. She approached one of the school governors. As a result, a new choir was formed called the school choir. I was the only girl who was in the school choir but not also in the chapel choir. Before I left St Felix, I sang in one concert with them, but I was never allowed to sing with the choir in the chapel.

There were happy moments—picnics in the summer at Thorpeness, visits to the Aldeburgh Festival, concerts at the school. I was always very proud of Nancy when she came down to visit. She seemed more glamorous and attractive than other girls' mothers. I played tennis in the summer and got to the finals of the singles tournament, but nerves overcame me because the headmistress was watching. I was beaten six love, six love.

I counted the days until the holidays, but as soon as I got home, I was overwhelmed by the usual misery—the feeling of worthlessness, loneliness, Nancy not liking me, Juliet ignoring me, Adam teasing me. I had nowhere to go and nobody to turn to. The atmosphere at home became unhappy too. I remember when I was 14, Geoffrey lying on the stairs crying, huge heaving sobs. Nancy had moved her bedroom upstairs to the nursery floor.

My only friend at home was our gorgeous dog, a black cocker spaniel called Ike. I used to lie on the floor and cuddle him and if I pretended to cry he would lick my face. Once he disappeared for two weeks and we thought he was lost for ever. But one morning, as we were getting ready for school, I heard yapping downstairs in the street and rushed down to find Ike with a broken rope attached to him. We were all delighted. Geoffrey was in tears. Later we discovered that Ike had been found by a pet shop in Camden Town. He had escaped and made his way home. A couple of years later, while on holiday from St Felix, I came home one day to be told by our cleaner, Ivy, that Ike had been run over and killed. His body was in the coal room by the front door. I didn't want to look. I was heartbroken. I had lost my only friend.

A painful memory is giving Nancy a parsnip for her birthday. This must have been quite soon after we came back to England after the war because Geoffrey was involved. We children were all expected to give Nancy a present for her birthday; I do not think we ever did this when we were in America. I racked my brain to find something that was original, amusing, and unusual. I came up with a parsnip—a vegetable I knew my mother hated. This seemed to fit the bill. I thought it would make everybody laugh and please my mother. I was mortified when my father took me aside and said that it wasn't a good enough present and that I must give my mother something else. He took me to a bookshop, and I chose a book about a Victorian educationalist. In retrospect, I see that in giving my mother a parsnip I was acting out my relationship with her. I was giving her what she seemed to want from me—what she hated most. Nancy hated parsnips and so this is what I gave her.

At school, Christianity was a continual presence. I loved the chapel services, the ceremony, and most of all the music—the organ voluntaries and the hymns. When I was about fifteen, I started to think about the implications of Christianity, and it all seemed to make sense to me. It fitted in with my own needs. Being rejected, scorned of men, the Christian myth resonated with me. It made sense of my unhappiness and gave me a feeling of purpose. I decided I would follow the path of the saints; then I would be loved and valued. I read everything I could find in the school library about St Teresa of Avila and other saints. When I was sure this was the way for me, I made an appointment to see Miss Williamson. I sat outside her room, wondering what to say.

As soon as I was summoned in, I blurted out, "I believe in Christ. I want to be a Christian."

She was taken aback and her first comment was, "You realise that this does not mean you can join the choir."

"Of course not," I replied. I had not even thought of it.

Miss Williamson suggested some books I should read and that was the end of it, as far as she was concerned. But for me it was the beginning of a quest to separate myself from the negativity and bad feelings put upon me by Nancy.

In the holidays, I went to St John's Wood Church. When I introduced myself to the vicar, Noel Perry-Gore, and told him I was Jewish, he said, "I am proud to have you in the church." He was always kind to me, and I sensed that I was particularly valued because I was so young. After a time, my parents realised I was serious about wanting to be baptised and sent me to see a rabbi so that I would know more about my Jewish heritage. But nothing the rabbi said changed my mind. I was determined to become a

Christian. I felt instinctively that this was the way to cast off the badness that surrounded me.

When I left school, I lived in Paris for six months. Nancy arranged accommodation for me in a flat in Neuilly belonging to a Mademoiselle who took in several English girls, which rather undermined the idea of learning French. A guide called Guislaine took us around Paris. After a few weeks, I broke away from the group and joined a course at the Sorbonne for *étrangers* where I met Mette, a glamorous Danish girl who was two years older than me. She had a boyfriend in Denmark and seemed to me sophisticated and grown up. I was proud to be her friend and spent happy times with her.

When I came home, after six months away, I was keen to see what had happened to my bedroom. When Juliet was in Paris, the year before, her bedroom had been redecorated with a new bed covering and dressing table. I assumed the same would happen for me. But to my disappointment, when I arrived home, nothing had changed. My bedroom was exactly as it had been before I left. I was very upset by this but did not dare ask Nancy why she hadn't done for me what she had done for Juliet.

Nevertheless, things started to look up around then, because I discovered I was quite pretty and boys were attracted to me. For the first time in my life, I felt one up on Juliet.

When I left school, my intention was to become a violinist. My mother arranged for me to have lessons at the Royal Academy of Music with David Martin, a pleasant, Canadian, leader of a well-known quartet. Each week I would wait outside his room for my lesson. The student before me was a brilliant violinist and, as I listened to him through the door, it dawned on me that I would never make the grade as a professional violinist. I longed for independence, to leave home and to earn a living. After a few months I decided to follow a different path and not pursue a career in music. I had no regrets about giving up the violin, all those hours of practice were depressing and lonely. It was a relief to stop.

I bought a book, *Teach Yourself to Type*, and soon became a proficient typist. I started working at the University of London Press in Warwick Square near St Paul's. I was thrilled to be earning money, and at being rather good at what I did. But soon I became bored. The manager, Mr Brown, was kind and helpful and encouraged me to apply to be a reader in the editorial department of their sister company, Hodder & Stoughton. Their response was positive, but they said I had to stay for a year at the University of London Press before they would consider taking me on.

That was a very tedious year which I thought would never end. It was not just copy typing that got me down. In charge of the typing pool was Esther Oaten, an infuriating, nitpicking woman, who spoke as if she was trying to hide her suburban origins. She found me annoying and did everything she could to put me in my place. I in turn was horrible to her. But I worked hard. I always turned up early and often stayed late to impress Mr Brown and show him I was serious in wanting promotion. He was true to his word and a year later I was transferred to the editorial department at Hodders.

It was my dream job. There were four readers under the editor, Elsie Heron, a dour woman from Northumberland who had a heart of gold, lived for her work, and looked after her staff like a mother hen. She was endlessly kind and encouraging to me and to all her staff. I remember one, called Patricia, who suffered from depression and would sit like a lump at her desk, doing no work. Elsie was supportive and kind towards her. It was a revelation to me that Elsie did not tell Patricia to "pull herself together".

The job involved taking a manuscript off the top of the pile, reading it and writing a report. What could have been more interesting and pleasurable? Occasionally we would write blurbs for the jacket of a book we had read. More advanced readers would edit books. This was what Elsie did mostly. I remember her working on John Hunt's book, *The Ascent of Everest*. One book I edited was an account by Andrzej Panufnik's first wife Scarlett about his escape from Poland. Because he was a musician, I was fascinated by it. I was good at my job. I remember Mr Ralph, as we called the Chairman, wrote a note saying, "Excellent report by Miss Raphael who has hit the nail on the head."

I bought a bike with a motor on the back to get to work. Geoffrey lent me the money to buy it. I used to pay him back in instalments each week after I had been paid. I remember he was surprised when I did this, as if he didn't expect me to honour my debt. He had become a rather peripheral figure in our lives at this time. He and Nancy rarely spoke. He slept in his dressing room, a small room with a bathroom beside it. Nancy slept upstairs in the room between Juliet's bedroom and mine.

Those three years, when I was working at Hodders, were very happy. Although I was still living at St Mark's Square, I was independent. My mother's indifference was, at that time, an advantage. I could decide how I wanted to live my life.

There were quite a few parties given by Jewish families in lavish surroundings to which Juliet and I were invited. It was fun dressing up in party dresses and great for my morale to know that I was pretty and admired by young men. But I was soon bored by the Jewish circle we were in; there were very few attractive men, most were very short, boring, and our conversations tended to be on subjects that didn't interest me. An exception was David Maitland, a distant cousin, who was 31, which seemed very old to me. He was quite tall and congenial. There was never a real spark between us, but I found his attention appealing—it was a feather in my cap to have a boyfriend who was 31. But after a bit, I became irritated by him; he was rather sentimental and would look at me with moon eyes. The final straw was when he said that when he and I got married, "we would unite the family silver."

After the relationship with David ended, I tried to join an amateur dramatic society in the hope of making new friends, but they told me they didn't need any more young girls in their plays.

Instead, I joined the St Johns Wood Choral Society, a small group that met in a church hall. I had always loved singing, and, ever since being banned from the choir at St Felix, had longed to sing in a choir. The conductor was Francis Routh, a tall, good-looking, ascetic young man. I sat in the front row of the altos and after a couple of rehearsals was desperately in love with him. His friends told me he was engaged to somebody else, but this didn't put me off. I did everything I could to get his attention; I was endlessly helpful, made sure I looked attractive, and took every opportunity to spend time with him.

Our first date was at St Paul's Cathedral to hear St Matthew Passion. Francis turned up an hour late and we missed the beginning of the performance. This did not put me off. Nothing mattered to me except that I should succeed in capturing him. When I did, I couldn't believe my luck in having this glamorous man as my boyfriend. Glamorous is not the right word. He was very attractive to me because he was tall and thin and, in true romantic style, was lean, hungry, had no money, and lived in one room in Courtfield Gardens, Earls Court. I loved his abrasive manner. I loved the way he ignored me when people were around but let me flirt and attract him when we were alone. I loved the way he confided in me about his life, his uncertainty about whether to be a conductor, composer, or an organist. I was convinced, as he was, that he was an unrecognised genius and that it was my task to nurture him and look after him.

The year that I fell in love with Francis, when I was 19, passed like a whirlwind. The only thing I could think about was him; everything revolved around my times with him, usually in his untidy little room in Courtfield Gardens. It was crammed with his possessions—on the floor, on the table, in the one cupboard. I was surprised one day to see on the top shelf in the cupboard some women's hats. "What are these?" "They're Barbara's". Barbara was the mystery fiancée who lived in Bristol. He never told me anything about her, but I knew of her existence through Francis's friends in the choir. She didn't make an appearance and he never mentioned her, until one day I was in his room with him when there was a knock on the door. A woman stood there, country-looking, older than me. It was Barbara. I was shocked to the core. I left in a hurry and went back to St Mark's Square. I felt my world had come to an end and I wanted to die. Geoffrey was there but I didn't say anything to him. I wonder if he noticed how upset I was.

A few hours later, the phone rang. It was Francis. He said that he had broken off his relationship with Barbara and he wanted to be with me. I was beside myself with joy. But the episode had shaken me. I knew Francis and Barbara had been lovers. She had lived with him for a time—hence the hats—and her appearance taught me that if I was going to hold onto Francis, I had to have sex with him. In those days this was a huge decision. Heavy petting was acceptable, intercourse was not. But I loved Francis so much I would do anything to keep him, even though it was against my Christian beliefs and my view of myself as a good person.

I asked Nancy about birth control. This was her speciality, as she was involved with the Family Planning Association. But not only this—she had very outlandish views about sex. She said to me once, "If you are still a virgin at 25, you should be ashamed of yourself!" So it was not difficult to broach the subject with her. She referred me to one of the Family Planning doctors, who lived in Regents Park. She was much more shocked than my mother and gave me a lecture about premarital sex. But that didn't deter me. Sex with Francis was great. This was him at his best—loving, gentle, attentive. The strange thing was that as soon as it was over, he reverted to his arrogant, uncaring self. I always felt that the Francis I knew in bed was the real man, and this is why I continued to love him for so many years, even though out of bed he treated me appallingly. But more of that later.

When Francis said he wanted to marry me, I always said I didn't want to—I was too young, I just wanted to enjoy life. "You will come round to it," he would say. And eventually I did. When I told my parents that I was going to marry Francis, a whole new dimension opened up. Having an affair with a penniless musician was one thing, but deciding to marry him was quite another. I don't know what went on in the background, but I expect there were a lot of phone calls and consultations among the family. Uncle Tom gave a party at his flat in Kensington for the family to meet Francis. I was very pleased to be the centre of attention. I was thrilled by the whole situation. Nancy seemed to be very pleased too. The only person who would have sounded a warning note was Geoffrey, but he was not at the party. He rarely took part in family occasions.

When we became engaged, Francis took me to meet his parents. They were a very nice, down-to-earth family. Pa was a headmaster, shortly to retire, at Guisborough Grammar School in Yorkshire. They lived in a large Victorian house that was next door to the school. Ma was a tall, thin woman, rather bent over with a hunch back and crippled legs so she walked rather badly. They were both very nice people and very kind and welcoming to me. Ma was a very clever woman. At breakfast, they would all sit round the table and do the Times crossword. She was the one who could do most of the clues. She was also, I believe, a talented pianist, though I never heard her play. Ma was always in the kitchen. She was the family drudge who did all the domestic duties, never complaining, only rarely venturing out of the kitchen, always stirring something on the stove. She was, in fact, a rather bad cook who produced disgusting soups made from the remains of everything, including Pa's breakfast porridge. But everybody loved her. She was a sort of saint but without in any way being sanctimonious. I remember she tried to warn me about Francis. She clearly loved him—he was after all her eldest son and it hurt her to say anything against him—but she said to me, "I must warn you, Francis can be very selfish." This didn't upset me. I thought, of course he's selfish, he is a musician—that is how they are.

THE PERFECT MARRIAGE

"YOU'RE MAKING AN awful mistake," Geoffrey said. "I know about people, and I can tell you that this man will not make you happy." Dear old Daddy, I thought. He hasn't a clue. He doesn't know Francis as I do.

At our wedding, the only jarring moment was in Francis' speech, when he said, "Virginia has put her money on a dark horse." Was my family's money the reason he had married me? I hastily brushed the thought away. Money was not a subject ever discussed in my family. But I knew my grandparents were wealthy and that my mother no longer worried about money as she had when we returned to London after the war. I was also aware that money was an issue between my parents. My father was proud of his achievements in his career and felt emasculated when he could not support the family on his salary alone and that we were reliant on my mother's money.

Francis and I began our marriage in two rooms, sharing a bathroom and kitchen with another couple on the top floor of 58

Courtfield Gardens. The owner was an eccentric guy who would often drop in to talk to us. The other couple, with whom we shared the bathroom and kitchen, had very noisy rows. I remember her shouting at him "Get out of my life!"

After about a year, we moved to a flat near Fulham Road. Francis worked in the front room, and there was a kitchen and bathroom, and two bedrooms. At that time Francis was teaching at Morley College and tutoring little boys so he was not at home all the time. Those days for me were a haze of uncertainty and insecurity. I didn't know anything about cooking or looking after a flat, and I felt very unsure of Francis because he never told me what he was doing and expressed little affection to me. As usual with me, when things aren't right, I blamed myself and tried a bit harder.

Simon was born in March 1958. I had been to antenatal classes and knew what to expect but it was quite a stressful experience, facing it on my own. In those days, husbands rarely stayed with their wives during the birth and in any case, I think it unlikely that Francis would have wanted to. After Simon was born, while I was still in hospital, something in me told me not to see my mother. She wanted to come to see him in the hospital—quite naturally, as Simon was her first grandson—but I was adamant I did not want her near him. Looking back, it seems a very strange reaction, because at that time I was always trying to be close to Nancy. When Francis applied for a job as an organist at the cathedral in Alberta, Canada, what upset me was the thought of being separated from her.

A few weeks later, this fear had gone and I was happy for Nancy to come to see Simon. She was a real help to me because she would take him out for a walk and this gave me some time for myself. When I look back on this episode, it seems very strange, my fear of letting my mother near my baby. It was as if I had a premonition of what was going to happen later on.

Simon was a wonderful little baby, very alert, attractive and responsive. I adored him but found looking after him very exhausting as he wouldn't sleep. I was not a good sleeper myself but whenever I did manage to fall asleep, I was woken by his cries. Francis was very pleased to have a son, but I cannot remember him doing anything to help—it was all left to me. This was not as shocking then as it is now. In those days, it was assumed that childcare was the preserve of women, as was cooking, cleaning, ironing, indeed all domestic duties. I was often at the end of my tether from exhaustion.

Francis was organist at a church in Redcliffe Gardens, quite near where we lived. He started a choral society there and I helped him by being the secretary to the choir. We had a series of babysitters to look after Simon so that I could attend the choir rehearsals. The vicar of the local church was very keen to have concerts in the church. I remember one concert: Nancy had brought two friends with her, one of whom was a music critic. I knew this was important for Francis. If the music critic was impressed by what he did, he would write a favourable review about him. As I sang in the choir facing the audience, I could watch the music critic's reaction. There was one false entry when Francis forgot to bring in one of the soloists. The music critic looked very unimpressed and I knew that nothing further would come of this.

At that time, Francis was wondering whether to pursue a career as an organist, conductor, or composer. But everything he tried to do ended in failure—not because of his ability, but chiefly because of his personality. He auditioned as an organist for the BBC. I remember being in the room while he talked on the telephone to one of adjudicators who said he was very impressed by the way Francis played at the audition. He asked Francis to return to play for another audition. At this one, they asked him what was in his repertoire. He cited eight different pieces. They asked him to play one of them, and as he hadn't practised it, he was unable to play it well. That was the end of his career as an organist, though he did apply, without success, for posts at the various cathedrals.

Though he was a competent choir conductor, and the choral society was a success, Francis became flustered when in a concert situation—as he had at the concert attended by the music critic – and therefore there was no mileage for him as a conductor.

Another project he was involved in was setting up the music department at Surrey University. This was because he taught an evening class at Battersea College of Technology which formed the basis of the new department at Surrey. Francis did not get on well with the head of department; there was a showdown between them when Francis was accused of plagiarism. He had written an article about Stravinsky, which the head of department said had been lifted from someone else's article. Francis was furious at the accusation, but the head of the department refused to back down. The two of them went to the Vice Chancellor who said Francis should leave. That was the end of his academic career. At this stage, I think I made the mistake of encouraging him to give up tutoring jobs so that he could concentrate on composition. I wanted things to go well for him, and most of all I wanted him to love me, and I thought that if all obstacles were removed, he would be able to forge ahead.

Another failure that comes to mind was over the new organ at St Philips Church in Earls Court. Francis was instrumental in getting this built by Noel Mander. My mother, who was always keen to help Francis in any way, suggested employing someone to publicise the new organ. This all went ahead without Francis telling Noel Mander. When he found out, he was furious and insisted that all the articles be withdrawn.

Two or three years after Francis and I were married, Francis's father spoke critically to me about Francis. I can't remember what he said but I know I reacted violently - not to him, but within myself. I realise now, looking back, that what Pa was saying, echoed what I myself was thinking unconsciously, but I couldn't allow myself to think critically of Francis at that time. Too much of my life was invested in him. He had to be the great artist, infallible, a good husband; our marriage had to be perfect. I repressed all my misgivings, all my unhappiness, and when Pa voiced his criticisms, it was intolerable. I was determined that my marriage would work. My parents had divorced in 1956 after many years of unhappiness. I wanted to show the world that my marriage was perfect—that I had an ideal husband and that everything in the garden was rosy.

As a result of his criticisms of Francis, I became allergic to Pa. I couldn't bear him, couldn't bear to be in the same room as him, disliked everything about him. Every three months, he came from Yorkshire to stay with us in London because he had been elected to the Church Assembly. Days before he arrived I would become worried and tense, and while he was with us, I could hardly look him in the face or talk to him. And, of course, I didn't sleep. I worried endlessly about my behaviour, and I couldn't understand why I hated him so. I knew that he was a nice man, kind, generous and loving. But I hated him and bristled at everything he said. I couldn't work out what it was about. I longed to find somebody who might help me. I knew Nancy had a friend who was a therapist and I tried to contact her. But maybe I had the wrong number. I was never able to get hold of her or find anyone to help me.

JOURNAL (May 1965) There must be a reason for this, yet I can't find it. As soon as he arrives, then I become a different person. Rigid, unhappy, tense, unable to look him in the face. It seems so absurd, he's such a well-meaning, kind man. Why, oh why, does he have this effect on me?

Francis is always just the same; his father's presence doesn't seem to worry him one way or another. And yet, in an odd way, although he is sympathetic with me about my feelings for his father, he seems to aggravate them, practically intentionally. For instance, this evening, Pa asked Francis to have lunch with him on Wednesday, then said "It would be nice if you could come too, Virginia." Francis said, "Yes, why don't you?" when he knew perfectly well it was the last thing I would like to do. So, I had to make excuses and I'm left feeling guilty.

Guilty—that is one of the worst things about Pa and me. I feel constantly guilty—horrible—and I deserve to feel guilty—because I am really absolutely beastly to him the whole time. I can't talk to him naturally, it's an effort to tell him anything, or to listen to him and, as I do so, it is as if a little voice somewhere behind me is continually criticising him. I keep on telling myself that I am being silly, selfish, inconsiderate, neurotic. Every time I behave in this way, I feel guilty. And yet I can't stop it. I make myself miserable (here I am in the middle of the night writing this) and I imagine I make Pa unhappy too. It's a great pity as he means so well, tries continually in such an open Christian way, to make amends. He must think me a most tiresome girl and so I am when he's around, but I don't think I am most of the time.

Ben was born in September 1959, eighteen months after Simon. Shortly before Ben was born, we moved to a larger flat in Notting Hill Gate. Simon was a very alert, attractive little boy, but he was never keen to go to sleep. Ben, by comparison, was a contented happy baby who went to sleep easily. I had a perfect family, I thought.

One day, when Ben was five months old, I was playing with him on my lap, bouncing him up and down on my knee, when I noticed that one of his legs didn't straighten. He did not seem in pain, but his knee was bent and he pressed on my lap with only one foot. I took him to the doctor the next day. She thought it was probably an infection and put him on antibiotics. After a week, his knee was still bent. She then referred him to the local hospital where he was admitted to the children's ward and put on stronger antibiotics. Still, there was no progress.

Francis was immersed in his work and hardly aware of what was going on. I knew nothing about the medical world or how to get an opinion from another consultant. But as the weeks progressed and Ben's condition did not improve, a friend of my mother's, George Stroh, a doctor and a child psychiatrist, offered to help. Following George's advice, I told our doctor we needed a second opinion. As a result, I took Ben to a consultant paediatrician at one of the London teaching hospitals. We were ushered into the consultant's room, and I introduced myself and explained the problem. The consultant laid Ben on a bed, took hold of his leg and tried to straighten it, causing him to scream with pain. It was horrifying. I left as soon as I could. I knew I did not want to see that doctor ever again. I contacted George to ask him what I should do. He then suggested I take Ben to see a consultant at University College Hospital.

As soon as I met Dr Bonham Carter at University College Hospital, I felt reassured that he knew what he was doing. He was able to make a diagnosis immediately. He said Ben had Still's disease, a form of rheumatoid arthritis in children. He said he would treat it with a new wonder drug, prednisone, a corticosteroid, and that this would stop the progression of the disease. Ben was admitted into the children's ward, where his leg was straightened under anaesthetic and put in a plaster cast. For me, it was a nightmarish time. I couldn't be in two places at once. I wanted to be with Ben in hospital, but Simon was a very demanding two-year-old and needed me at home. I had recently passed my driving test and was very apprehensive about driving in London on my own. Ben's illness forced me to drive every day, as I could only get to the hospital by car. We were fortunate to find an au pair, who was able to look after Simon while I was at the hospital.

Although I thought Ben was in good hands, as the weeks progressed I worried about him. He was not thriving in hospital. He was a sociable baby and needed company, but for some reason they kept him in a separate room away from the other children on the ward. He would have been much happier if he had been in the main ward. When I arrived each day, I would see a sad little boy, lying staring into space, nothing to amuse him, nothing to stimulate him. I was aware that he was deteriorating psychologically. Also, physically he was not in good shape. His face had become moon-shaped, a side effect of the steroids, and he had a sore at the top of his leg where the plaster cast rubbed against his skin.

In August, five months after Ben became ill, we planned a holiday in the Isle of Wight and I wanted to have Ben with us. I couldn't bear to leave him alone in hospital, sad and withdrawn. I knew he needed stimulation and company and I thought being part of the family would give him that. When the time for our holiday arrived, the consultant was on leave. I said to the young doctor in charge that I could look after Ben at home, and I wanted to take him with us on holiday. The young doctor was not happy about this but I insisted.

We had a happy time with Ben on the Isle of Wight. I remember him sitting in his pram on the beach saying "ohh-ba" with a huge grin. The day after we came back to London, Ben started to breathe in a strange way. I took him to the hospital immediately and was greeted by a doctor whom I didn't know, who said that I should never have taken Ben out of hospital in the first place. They put him on oxygen and he seemed to settle so I went home. In the middle of the night there was a phone call from the hospital. Ben had collapsed. They said we should come in immediately. With Francis driving, we rushed across London as fast as we could. But when we arrived at the hospital, Ben had died. I sat with him in his bleak single room. His little face looked crumpled and sad.

Later, I learnt that his death was caused by too high a dosage of steroids. Today, the recommended treatment for Still's disease is aspirin. As it was, he was the youngest child they had ever treated for Still's disease and they got the dosage wrong. Often Still's disease burns itself out and the child, though sometimes disabled by it, is able to live a normal life. If Ben had lived today, he might have been disabled by Still's disease, but he would not have died.

When we got back to our flat in Notting Hill Gate that evening, Francis and I sat together in the sitting room and cried for most of the night. I remember thinking then that we were closer than we had ever been. I clung onto the hope that out of the disaster of Ben's death, our marriage would come to life. But this closeness didn't last. Francis went back to his solitary absorption in himself and his work. I became numb with pain and misery. There was nobody to talk to. The only person who showed their support was my grandmother who came to London specially to take me out. After treating me to lunch in a luxury restaurant, she bought me a fur coat. It was her way of showing sympathy. I found most people unable to cope with my grief. They would cross the road to avoid me.

One notable exception was George Stroh and his wife Katrin who invited us to stay with them in their holiday house in Dartington. Ben died on the thirteenth of August. We three, Francis, Simon and me, went to stay with the Strohs on the twentieth when the Dartington Festival was at its peak and they took us to concerts and talks. We stayed with them for a week. Dartington seemed a magical place to me. It was a community set up by the visionary, Leonard Elmhirst, who had married an American heiress, Dorothy Payne Whitney. It was in a beautiful part of the world, and the people we met there seemed glamorous and unconventional. I was excited by Dartington. The whole concept of a utopian community was inspiring to me. Even through my numbness, I could sense the vibrancy of the place.

After Ben died, there was a huge gap in our family. Before, we had seemed a perfect little unit, Francis, me and the two little boys. Now there was a gaping hole. I thought the only solution was to have another baby. I became pregnant very quickly and Tina was born the following year, in July 1961. But, as any psychologist would have told me, this was not the way to overcome my grief about Ben's death. When Tina was born, we were thrilled to have a little girl. Although I thought Tina was the most beautiful baby, I had lost my confidence in being a mother. I was frightened all the time that she wouldn't survive. I felt I was a bad mother because I hadn't been able to keep Ben alive. Deep within me was the feeling that I had been responsible for his death.

I didn't face my feelings of grief and despair about the loss of Ben for many years. I threw myself into work. The family trust gave us an annual income, but we were always short of money. Francis earned very little and what he did, he kept for himself. Therefore, I needed to earn money, but my frenetic working pattern was in order to escape myself.

I had continued working at Hodders until Simon was born. Then I became a part-time reader for them. Once a week, I would go into the office to pick up manuscripts, which I would read at home. I would write reports and bring back the manuscripts the following week. This fitted in well with looking after Simon, but after a time I began to miss the company of the others. It was lonely at home; even though Francis was there most of the time, he was not around to talk to. At that time, it was easy to get childcare and I employed a series of au pairs.

In 1962, when Tina was a toddler and Simon was four, I met an unusual woman called Joan Wilkins, who had a shop in Parkway, Camden Town, and from it ran an agency called "Freelance Work for Women". Joan Wilkins was a charismatic, dotty women in her fifties – impossible to work for, but fun to be with. I joined her in running the agency and working in the shop.

After a year, I moved on to a job as a conference organiser at the Town and Country Planning Association. This was a very busy office and among the conferences were a series on leasehold reform. My job was to organise conferences for lawyers all over England to explain the legislation.

At that time, homelessness became a big issue following a very successful TV drama *Cathy Come Home*. A Methodist minister, Bruce Kenrick, had started Shelter, a charity for the homeless. When I met him one evening at a dinner party, he invited me to join Shelter as office manager. This new project excited me, and I wanted to help Bruce. I thought I could keep my job at the Town and Country Planning Association ticking over while I put all my energies into getting Shelter off the ground. This was not a good idea. Trying to do both jobs at the same time was unsatisfactory for both organisations and very exhausting for me. My life was one manic whirl as I tried to juggle all the elements in it. Although I had an au pair at home looking after Simon and Tina, I couldn't sustain the pace. I became ill with what I thought was flu, but after a week, two weeks, a month, I wasn't better. The doctor said she thought I had one of the diseases of the central nervous system and referred me to the hospital for nervous diseases in Queen Square.

During those weeks, as I waited for the appointment at the hospital, I stayed in bed, listened to music, and felt surprisingly contented and at peace—surprising, because I was so different from my previous restless self. One day, as I lay there, I saw suspended in the corner of the room, opposite the bed, where the cornice meets the ceiling, a luminous cross, gold and shining. I lay there looking at it—it seemed for hours—and felt supremely happy. Then I saw another image, a church on a hill, and I had an overwhelming feeling that I had to build that church.

At the hospital, the consultant told me I did not have one of the diseases of the central nervous system. My condition was caused by myxoedema, an under-active thyroid and could easily be treated by thyroxine. I recovered quickly and soon I was back to my usual energetic self. But I was not the same person as I had been before I became ill. I felt that the visions had changed me. I knew the church on the hill and the cross were important symbols. I knew they were speaking to me, but I misinterpreted them by taking them literally. At that time, I knew nothing about symbols or psychology. I thought the visions were telling me that my task was to build a real church on a real hill. I remembered Dartington, the utopian community, where we had stayed after Ben had died, and to me, it seemed an ideal place to do this.

I contacted one of the trustees of Dartington, Maurice Ash, who was on the council of the Town and Country Planning Association, where I had been working. After I explained to him why I wanted to live at Dartington, he invited Francis and me to stay for the weekend. We made the long drive to Devon at the beginning of May. When we arrived at Maurice's house, in Ashprington, near Dartington, I couldn't believe my eyes. Sharpham House was a majestic Palladian house above the Dart valley; and on the lawn, overlooking the view, was a huge Henry Moore statue. I had never before stayed in such grand surroundings. Maurice and his wife Ruth greeted us. He was a very warm, approachable man; Ruth was shy but made an effort to be friendly to us. I didn't know Maurice well and he had never told me that he lived in such grandeur. I learnt that Ruth was the daughter of Leonard and Dorothy Elmhirst, the founders of Dartington.

Francis and I both felt overwhelmed by our surroundings, but it affected us in different ways. I tried to be helpful and charming and fit in with Maurice and Ruth. But Francis became withdrawn and silent, and I could see that this gave a bad impression. On Saturday evening, as we were dressing for dinner, my frustration with Francis burst out.

"It's hopeless. It's not going to work," I said to him, through tears.

"What on earth is the matter?"

"You always kick gift horses in the mouth," I said, sobbing.

Francis said wearily, after a pause, "For goodness sake! What are you talking about?"

"You know that I want to move to Dartington. You know why it's so desperately important for me. . ."

"I can't change my whole life because you've had a hunch," said Francis.

I knew that what repelled Francis more than anything about the idea of moving to Dartington was the religious overtones of my "hunch," as he called it. I could understand his reaction; but the urgency in me could not be dispelled. I knew I had to somehow get through to him. Some way or other, I had to persuade Francis of the logic of moving to Dartington, the rightness of it. I begged him to lower his guard so that people could get to know him.

Maurice had arranged an eventful weekend to introduce us to key figures in the Dartington community. We met members of the Dartington quartet, the head of the music and several people from the art college. On Sunday, Maurice and Ruth gave a lunch party for us. The guests included a British composer, Alun Hoddinott, and Jack Dobbs, head of music at the college. Francis made an effort, but I could see that his arrogant way of talking did not make a good impression. Maurice could not have done more to help us. But Francis's superior manner made me feel despairing, as I recounted in my journal two weeks later.

JOURNAL (June 1969) Where have we got to since I last wrote? Nowhere. And that is, I suppose, where we are going to stay, unless a miracle happens. We went to Dartington—Francis behaving in a stiff, unapproachable way. Maurice, puzzled, made every possible effort to help.

Yes, Francis likes the place, would not object to move there, but will only go if there is a job to go to. And will there be? Very unlikely, because Francis writes stiff, arrogant letters to Jack Dobbs, head of music, which can do nothing but antagonise. So chances are minimal.

Am I wrong in wanting to move to Dartington? Is this just a craze of mine? Why can't I let go of the idea? Why does it matter so desperately to me? Everything in London seems dreary and pointless. I can only think of Dartington and long and long to be there. Is this God urging me on or an obsession that is needling me? How to know? I dread more than anything being condemned to a life of limbo—a life of nothingness—and that is what I see in London. Yet I am tied, bound to Francis. If he will not move, here I must stay. But I long—long—long to go to Dartington. Selfish, neurotic, is this what I am? It would be so much easier if I were. Because I could pray and overcome it. But the more I pray—the more I long for Dartington. Oh God, help me. What can I do?

The images from the visions were always on my mind, but because I interpreted them literally, I was banging my head against a wall. I later came to understand that the visions indicate the beginning of individuation: the cross and the church suggest that the task would be spiritual; the hill suggests that the journey would be arduous. Although I did not understand them or what was happening to me, these three symbols—the cross, the church, and the hill—inspired and propelled me forward.

I started to look at my life and to consider what mattered to me. I realised that the children were the most important part of my life. I had not been a good mother. I had always been in a hurry, always wanting to do something else, never just being at peace and enjoying the children. I also realised that the sort of jobs I had been doing were not satisfying. I wanted to do something different— something that would help other people but not jeopardise my relationship with the children. I made two huge decisions. The first was to have two more children—and this time I would really enjoy them and spend time with them. The second was to train as a marriage guidance counsellor. Several of my friends were doing this and I had heard about the training from them. It only required five hours a week and a weekend course every six months, which would fit in well with the children. At that time my income from the family trust had increased so we were no longer dependent on what

I earned. We were not well off—we could not afford luxury items or holidays—but we had enough to live on. Where was Francis in all this? I don't remember discussing any of my plans with him. For him, children, household, what I spent my time doing, were my concern, not his.

Going to church had been a very important part of my adult life. But after I had the visions, my attitude changed in a way I found very bewildering. If I went to church, I would feel tense and nauseous. During the service, I wanted to stand up and shout, "This is rubbish, this isn't right, you do not understand what you're talking about!" This violent aversion to religion, and in particular church services, started in 1969, after I had the visions. It wasn't that I went off religion. Indeed, I still cared passionately about it— but I couldn't accept what was on offer.

It was Jung who helped me to understand what was happening to me. I have a vivid memory of when this occurred. I was lying in bed, recovering from flu and reading *Memories, Dreams, Reflections,* my first introduction to Jung. I came to the section where Jung says that after he experienced the numinous power of the unconscious, the church's message seemed innocuous and flawed. "Yes!" I shouted out loud as I read this. His words spoke directly to me. I knew then that this was the route I wanted to follow.

Thus began my journey of exploration. Reading Jung helped me to come to terms with spirituality by translating religious words into psychological words. The religious terminology that had been part of my vocabulary since becoming a Christian at 16, was replaced by psychological words. I could no longer follow the religious route, therefore I listened to my inner voice and followed my personal path. Now, looking back, I can see the similarities of the two. Theology and psychology both point to the spiritual dimension, but use different terminology.

The birth of Belinda in 1970 and Alexander in 1972 were joyous events. I loved being a mother and found great contentment in my relationships with these two adorable children. The effect their arrival had on the rest of the family was also salutary. As a young child, Simon had been stormy and difficult, chiefly, I think, because of Ben's death. Ben was eighteen months younger than Simon. I knew nothing about child psychology in those days. I did not realise how much the baby's death had affected Simon. The new life in our family brought out the best in Simon and Tina. As Simon grew up, he became a very strong minded, focused boy who knew what he wanted to do. He often held the fort at home if I was delayed at work and there would be a happy atmosphere when I arrived. I remember him paying Belinda and Alexander to iron his shirts. Tina was very good at craft and taught the little children how to do patchwork.

My mother and Francis got on very well together, they buttered each other up and enjoyed each other's admiration. I dreaded being with the two of them. They would chat away together and ignore me. One year, on my birthday, when we were out at a restaurant, I was so exasperated by this that I considered walking out—picking up my coat and handbag and going home on my own, leaving them to their mutual admiration. Would they even notice, I wondered? I didn't do it. I didn't have the courage, because by doing so I would be cast as the "bad girl," as I had been throughout my childhood. I was caught in a trap between husband and mother. For years, I didn't acknowledge this. I knew I was tense and unhappy, I knew I had problems sleeping, I knew I was mixed up, but I didn't know why.

My mother doted on Simon and made life difficult for me by implying I was the bad mother and she was the good mother. She indulged Simon and invited him to many prestigious events—the opera at Covent Garden and Glyndebourne—and would take him with her to visit her friends. Simon loved this. Granny was a very important part of his life. But for me and for the family, it was very divisive. Christmas was often painful for me because Simon was with my mother at my sister's house rather than at home with us.

Tina was a beautiful little girl and very bright. "You're very lucky to have a daughter like Christina," her teacher said when Tina started school at five. I was puffed up with pride. When Belinda and Alexander were born, we were living in a flat in Notting Hill Gate. Mrs Morris came to help with the cleaning soon after Belinda was born, and she became an essential prop of my life. She was a young Irish woman with three children of her own and I felt very confident leaving the children with her.

Because Mrs Morris was at home to look after the children, I was able to start the training for marriage guidance counselling in 1973, when Alexander was one and Belinda was three. It was an excellent training which I found thought-provoking and stimulating. It provided many insights into myself, though it did not enable me to examine my own marriage. For me, it was still the perfect marriage with the perfect husband.

Soon afterwards, we moved out of the flat in Notting Hill Gate to a house in Chiswick, bought by the family trust. We lost Mrs. Morris as a helper, a devastating blow, and I was never able to replace her. I juggled the pieces of my life as best I could. I cleaned the house myself and had one free afternoon a week when my mother played with the children for a couple of hours. When Belinda and Alexander started full-time school, I had quite a lot of time for my own activities. In the holidays, I looked after my friends' children in return for them looking after mine. Although Francis worked at home, he was not willing to look after the children or to give them tea after school. But as the children grew older, the fact that he was on the premises, in the studio in the garden, reassured me that he would be there if a crisis arose.

In 1975, when I was 40, I showed my mother a copy of the novel I had been writing on and off for a few years. I was always wanting my mother's approval, but her reaction was not at all what I expected. *Marking Time* was about a young woman living in Chelsea who had an unhappy marriage. Nancy assumed that I was writing about myself. I wasn't consciously doing this, but, as a result of reading it, Nancy offered to pay for me to have analysis.

"It's very generous of you, Mum." I couldn't help feeling flattered at her attention and her offer to pay. For a long time, I had been intrigued by psychology, psychoanalysis and the whole mystery surrounding mental illness. My mother's offer not only solved the financial problem (we couldn't afford it) but also gave the whole idea legitimacy. I knew Francis would not like it. The world of the psyche, for him, was akin to the world of the occult. Our marriage was based on his dominance and my subservience. I knew he would oppose me having analysis because it would make me stronger and disturb the equilibrium in our relationship. But my mother was a force to be reckoned with. Because she had suggested it, he was unable to stop it. He valued her good opinion of him and did not want to oppose her.

Why did my mother suggest it? At the time I thought she was being kind and generous. Now I see it very differently. By offering to pay for my analysis, Nancy was making herself feel better. I was the shadow part of her psyche, the part that pulled her down and made her depressed. For Nancy, I was the troublesome member of the family, the one onto whom she dumped all the negativity in herself. I was the dustbin for all her bad feelings. By paying for analysis for me, she was attempting to heal the damaged part of herself. From the beginning, Nancy made sure that she controlled the analysis, first by insisting that my analyst should be her close friend and former analyst, Faye Pye, and second, saying that the bills for the analysis should be sent to her and not given to me.

FAYE

I KNEW NOTHING about analysis. I didn't know what I should talk about, what was relevant, what was not. But I was very excited at the prospect of this new venture. For me, analysis was a lifeline. Instinctively I knew this was the route out of the trap I was in, although at that stage I did not know I was in a trap. All I knew was that, like the heroine in the novel I had written, I was unhappy, unfulfilled, and unable to sleep. If anybody had asked, I would have said that I had a husband I adored, a happy family, and I didn't understand why I was so mixed up.

The most important hour of the week for me was Tuesday afternoons from two to three. This was the time of my analytic session with Faye. I counted the days to it. It required considerable organisation to get there on time. I had to arrange childcare for Belinda and Alexander and take public transport across London to Harley Street. The journey took me about an hour. Then there was a long walk from the underground station to Faye's consulting room. I studied the brass plates advertising the prestigious doctors as I walked along the road, rehearsing in my mind what I was going to say to Faye.

Faye's consulting room was on the fourth floor of an imposing building. Before I started analysis, I knew what Faye looked like because she frequently chaired meetings at the Jung club. My mother often took me to lectures there. Faye was an elderly woman, plump, short grey hair. She was always dressed in the same outfit— trousers, long waistcoat, and beads around her neck. She was kind to me, and listened to what I had to say, but at the end of the 50-minute session I often felt dissatisfied. I hadn't expressed what was bursting inside me. I sensed that I was on the edge of territory I wanted to explore but I did not know how to get there.

From the beginning, one hour a week was not enough for me. I wrote copiously in my journal to express all the things that were bubbling up in me, things I wanted to say to Faye.

JOURNAL (July 1975) When you say you want to get to know me—I don't want to show you the me as in other relationships—the outside me—talking about externals—as I would with anybody. I want to explore the inside me—I want to show you the me that I don't know myself—to step through the glass door into the depths of me. I don't want to talk about Francis, the children, my past life—I want to talk about my feelings, fears. . . Not the flowers and leaves, but the rhizome I want to look at.

I seem split—part of me wanting to dream again, to explore further; another part of me feeling raw, exposed, frightened of going to sleep.

Wanting to impress, wanting to be unique. Feeling of importance, of having something special to offer, dissatisfaction with present, need to strive, to go forward. *folie de grandeur*— 40-year-old housewife who feels she has something important to offer, to discover.

Fantasy—that I shall so impress Faye that she will tell my mother what a splendid person I am—and then Mum will love me as much as the others.

The need to impress and the need to be impressive—talking dogmatically because of fear of being grey and boring. Even with my children, I find myself taking centre stage, unless I guard against it.

Ambition is a mixture of "look at me, see how clever I am, love me" and a need to stretch my abilities to see how far they will go. Like a corrosive acid, it eats through one position and strives onto the next.

The need to topple authority and see its clay feet, to take its place and do its job better. Competing, to be better than others, too painful to be less good than them. Caring and sympathetic to underdogs, dislike of top dogs.

Ambition didn't start until I married? I'm not ambitious for Francis—frightened of success for him because he might leave me. It's a need only for the inside me. It seems to me that there are two elements in me and they have become muddled together—I need to clarify them. On the one side, there is the need to assert myself, due to my experience as a child. On the other side, my own abilities and personality pushes forward relentlessly with an energy of its own towards fulfilment and recognition.

Fear of the dark/mice/unknown things/of being out of control/of my own madness—balanced by the fact that I am courageous. If I know something needs to be done, I will do it, even if I'm afraid of the consequences.

"The unconscious is a process. . .The psyche is transformed or developed by the relationship of the ego to the contents of the unconscious." (Jung) The alchemists realised the purpose of their work was not the transmutation of base metals into gold, but the production of an *aurum non vulgi*—i.e. spiritual values and psychic transformation.

Not boring to her—but boring to the real me.

Last night, I had a dream about looking for a lavatory before going for analysis. I think the dream is saying to me that I must sort out my neurotic problems on my own and use the analytic time for the more important work. I must put my neuroses out of the way so they will not distract me.

How much is genuine? How much wish fulfilment? I now feel that the dream was saying that essential preparation is necessary before analysis can begin. It seems to me there are two areas I need to work through—my ambition and feelings about my own sexuality.

"The best analyst in London." This is how Nancy described Faye. I was proud to be in analysis with her. I knew Faye was much respected in the Jungian world. But there was an additional bonus. As she was a friend of my mother's, I thought that, at last, I would be valued and appreciated by Nancy—Faye would tell her what a splendid person I was. Therefore, from the beginning the analysis was flawed. I saw Faye as a channel to my mother. Faye saw me as Nancy's daughter. I was truly caught in a spider's web.

In most analytic relationships, the analyst is anonymous. He doesn't talk about himself and the patient does not know anything about the analyst's life. I knew quite a lot about Faye's life because my mother often talked to me about her. I knew she had recently married a dear old bumbler called Arnold, who tended to get drunk at Jung club parties. She never had children; her analysands were her children, the Jungian world her life. I knew she was involved in starting the training scheme for the Association of Jungian Analysts (AJA) and I knew that she was immersed in a feud with Gerhard Adler over the chairmanship of the organisation. I never mentioned any of this in the sessions, but these facts were in my mind. I thought, at the time, it was an advantage to know these things about Faye. Now, I can see it created a barrier in the analytic relationship. As a result of what my mother told me, it was as if other people were in the consulting room with me. It was never a closed container of Faye and me, analyst and patient, as it should have been.

"You're not going to see that quack again, are you?" Francis's words rang in my ears as I travelled across London. I told Faye that Francis had doubts about me having analysis. She offered to see him with a view to reassuring him. I don't know what she said to him—he didn't tell me and she never mentioned it—but he stopped calling her a quack and accepted the fact that I was going to see her on a regular basis.

My analytic sessions, once a week to begin with, then twice a week after a year, were the most important events in my life. I dreamt prolifically and recorded the dreams in a notebook I kept beside the bed. When life events were particularly painful, I wrote a journal as well. I would take my dream book along to the analytic sessions, and sometimes I would read one to Faye. But I never told her about the visions. At that time, they didn't seem relevant.

Here is the first dream I took to Faye.

DREAM Our house is going to be invaded by Indians—Francis and I get ready—we leave children in bed—and I make plans to hide in cupboard by the boiler—I hide my bag in case they take it. Before they come, I go to lav—and then before I have time to get back into my safe cupboard, a dark shadowy figure comes to the back door. I don't know if I'm going to have time to get back into my cupboard.

This dream foretells the work in analysis. It shows fear of contact with the unconscious (the Indians) and fear of being overwhelmed by it. It also shows a resilient ego that is taking action to defend itself. Going to the lav suggested the need psychologically to get rid of 'shit'—the negative stuff I was carrying. This first dream shows the beginning of individuation, when the conscious ego makes contact with the unconscious. In the four years I worked with Faye, there were indications of individuation in many of my dreams, but Faye did not recognise the symbolism, therefore I did not assimilate and learn from the dreams. The process of individuation was aborted each time it emerged.

There was a very painful episode during that time with Faye that stands out in my memory. Jung club meetings were very important events in my life. They took place once a month at a hall in Notting Hill Gate. Usually, one of the analysts gave a talk and I would look forward to these events with great enthusiasm. There was one given by Neil Micklem—a good looking man in his 50s. Something about his talk infuriated me, maybe not fulfilling my expectations or maybe his rather facile approach. Afterwards, I talked on the telephone about it to my mother. She had missed the lecture and I described it to her and my frustration about the evening. She said, "You must write to tell him. He should know how disappointed you were." So, I did.

A few weeks later, in my analytic session, Faye brought up the letter I had written to Neil Micklem. He had shown it to her because he considered it offensive. I had applied to be a member of the club but, because of the letter, he didn't want me to be accepted. After this session with Faye, when I was back at home, I shut myself in the lavatory and sat on the floor with my arms around my knees, rocking backwards and forwards to assuage the appalling psychic pain I was feeling. I felt as if a knife had been stuck in my heart. It was upsetting to be blackballed by the Jung club, but that in itself was not the cause of my pain. It was Faye becoming the punitive mother. It did not occur to me then that she was in any way at fault. I thought Neil Micklem was a vain man and a prat to react to my critical letter in the way that he did, but here was I, Virginia, the difficult one, mucking up things once again. It did not occur to me at that time that Nancy had goaded me into this situation.

During those four years with Faye, I had a striking dream about initiation, in which I am processing up the aisle of Westminster Abbey. All the other people in the procession are holding red umbrellas. I try to follow their example, but my umbrella has a broken spike. The dream is telling me that the initiation is the beginning of the individuation process; the broken spike in my umbrella suggests I am wounded and this needs to be addressed. At this time, there were also many dreams about eggs, some swinging in the wind and then crashing onto the ground. The egg symbolises the Self—the potential in each one of us—but in those years with Faye, the eggs always smashed. The following dream is critical of Faye and is telling me that I have to take a decisive step and look after myself.

DREAM A boarding house for ill people. Nurse shows me shrivelled up little man—she says he is only 18 months old but has been starved by his mother. She puts him to sleep in a cupboard under the stairs. I remonstrate—say it's not good enough for him. She lets me take him to another room. I hold him in my arms and play with him and love him and shortly he comes to life—and becomes like a normal baby.

When I look back on those years, I perceive so many missed opportunities because Faye was tangled up in the relationship with my mother and consequently didn't see me. Also, the feud with Gerhard Adler about the training scheme for AJA consumed a lot of her thoughts and energy. However, Faye gave me a priceless tool: she showed me how to work with my dreams. When she became ill and stopped working, although the break from her seemed devastating at the time, it proved a wonderful opportunity because I was able to work on my own and, from that time, individuation took off.

After Faye became ill and I began working on my own, I often consulted the *I Ching* when I had difficult decisions to make. Faye had introduced me to the ancient oracle and suggested I buy Richard Wilhelm's book on the *I Ching* which has a foreword by Jung. In it, Wilhelm explains the technique for consulting the oracle—either by using yarrow sticks or throwing coins. In those days, when I consulted the *I Ching*, I would write the problem I was struggling with at the top of the page, and then, following Wilhelm's instructions, I would divide the yarrow sticks, once, twice, several times, until one or two hexagrams emerged. I would then read and consider the opaque Chinese verse. Often it seemed to speak directly to my condition. Today, I use an excellent app on the phone which follows the same procedure but is easier to use.

BRUNEL

SOON AFTER I started analysis with Faye, I realised that I wanted to progress from being a counsellor to becoming an analyst. But before I could even apply for the analytic training, I had to get a degree: the training schemes would only accept university graduates and I had no formal qualifications. School had been problematic for me because I could not concentrate. "How can I be nicer? How can I be more like Juliet and Adam so that Nancy will love me as she does them? What's wrong with me? What can I do to put it right?" Round and round these worries circulated in my head and I was unable to listen to teachers: I switched off automatically as soon as they started talking, Therefore, I left school at 17 with no formal qualifications.

The prospect of doing a degree course excited me. I had always felt inferior intellectually to people with degrees, and to Francis in particular. London University would not accept me without any qualifying A-levels. But I discovered that Brunel University at Uxbridge, which was only half an hour's drive from Chiswick where we were now living, would accept me as a mature student with no qualifications. The Brunel course was a Bachelor of

Science honours course in psychology. It was a thrilling prospect but, predictably, Francis was adamantly against the idea.

"Why bother your little head with academic stuff? It will bore you. You'll get fed up with it. And who will look after the children?"

There followed a stormy few months. I was determined to go to Brunel and Francis was equally determined that I shouldn't.

I hated the tension between Francis and me and I couldn't bear the thought of the quarrelling and sniping going on once I had started the university course, but I couldn't see how to persuade Francis to change his mind. I discussed the problem with Faye who suggested we go to see a counsellor together. She gave me the name of an elderly clergyman whom she thought would be able to help us. Now, looking back, it seems extraordinary that Francis agreed to come with me to see the counsellor. But he did and the session was very helpful. The counsellor encouraged Francis to express his worries and doubts about me going to university. By the end of the session, he had helped Francis to see that furthering my education would not threaten our marriage.

Brunel's campus was not attractive. White square buildings made from concrete were situated on a bleak site with gas works in the background. It was early days when I was there; Brunel University had only been built ten years previously, and the landscaping hadn't become established, so it seemed bare and windswept. The lecture theatre building was square with an entrance on each side. I was always getting lost because I would go in one entrance and not realise I had come out of another.

I started at Brunel in September 1977, pencils sharpened, new loose-leaf folders, even a new car to get me there each day. Although I looked forward to the course, I also had worries. Would I be out of my depth? Would I understand what they were talking about? I was quickly both reassured and disillusioned. There were sixty students in my year, of which five were mature students. No Bertrand Russell among them. I soon realised, by the way they responded in seminars, that the young ones were not very bright and that the older students were earnest and boring. In seminars, they always asked "Will this be in the exam?" They didn't seem interested in psychology, only in getting through exams to gain their degree. The content of the course and the quality of the teaching were equally disillusioning. Subjects such as motivation and perception didn't interest me, although I made a prodigious effort to understand them. My interest was in psychodynamic psychology and there was very little in the course, and the little there was related to Freud.

It seemed strange to me that Jung was not mentioned in any of the lectures or in any of the required reading. How does Jungian psychology fit in with academic psychology, I wondered, and why is it ignored? It was not until the third year that I found the answer. A course that excited me was the history of scientific ideas, particularly Thomas Kuhn's seminal book, *The Structure of Scientific Revolutions*. He describes how science develops within paradigms, assumptions that are subscribed to by the scientific community. When new ideas come along, they often break the paradigm, causing conflict and discord. Kuhn cites Galileo as an example of someone whose revolutionary ideas broke an existing paradigm. For me, this was a revelation—a breath of fresh air, which explained why Jung's ideas were not generally accepted. I began to understand that Jung's discoveries did not fit into the existing paradigm of rationality and evidence-based science, because he had introduced the concept of the collective unconscious.

A course in my third year by John Odling Smee on evolution helped me fit Jungian psychology into mainstream academic psychology. Odling Smee's basic premise was that Darwin's theory of evolution had omitted learning and behaviour. In his lectures, he explained how the ability to learn fitted into the evolutionary framework. I could see that what he was talking about was the collective unconscious, though his terminology was different from

Jung's. It was exciting and reassuring to realise that what I was learning academically and what I was learning about myself psychologically were inextricably linked.

Although I found a lot of the lectures and seminars turgid and boring, I loved the academic work and spent every evening, after the children had gone to bed, writing essays and reading required texts. University fitted in very well with family life. During the term time I would take Belinda and Alexander to school and then drive on to Brunel which was only half an hour's drive from our home. University was never stressful for me in relation to the children because I had no responsibility there. Being a student was much easier than being an employee. Nobody minded if I didn't turn up or if I was late. When I missed a lecture or seminar, because of some problem at home, I would ask one of the students if I could copy their notes. There was a crèche at the university where I took Belinda and Alexander on a few occasions, but they hated it because by this time they were seven and five and they pointed out to me that the crèche was meant for babies.

JOURNAL (April 1980) What is giving me great joy at the moment is my new-found ability to write. For the first time for years, I feel free to write fluently—instead of doubt, uncertainty, and a hesitant, stilted, constipated sort of writing. I can now write a letter quickly and fluently. Once I know what I want to say, I can say it.

Brunel gave me far more than the opportunity to develop my intellectual ability, it provided a canvas on which my struggles with individuation were played out. The concept of the animus was foremost in my mind. What was it? How did it work? My dreams addressed the problem and, as I turned the dreams over and over in my mind, I began to understand the animus part of me. Predominant in many of my dreams was an assertive middle-aged man with grey hair who was always throwing his weight around and interrupting people. He seemed very ambitious and was determined to get a first class honours degree. I realised he was my animus, the masculine assertive part of me which often dominated how I behaved, without me realising it. I would shoot my mouth off when I was with other people; I was often abrasive and unintentionally upset people because my animus had me in his grip. As I worked with my dreams and started to recognise him, the animus no longer dominated the way I behaved. I started to cooperate with him. I also realised I often behaved inappropriately and in an unhelpful way because of the animus. I saw that my competitiveness and my readiness to throw myself into work, my enthusiasm, my single-mindedness (I had been told that I was like a terrier that wouldn't let go once I got hold of something) were animus qualities. I was often impatient, voracious for stimulating ideas, longing to find someone I could sharpen my wits against—all of which I came to realise can be negative animus if unconscious, but a positive and creative animus, if I was conscious of it and co-operated with it.

JOURNAL (May 1980) Today it struck me that what makes things difficult for me at Brunel is my animus. There is something heavy, insensitive and unrelated about my functioning. I don't seem to be able to blend thinking and feeling—can it be done? If I concentrate on relatedness (as I do with patients) there is a warm feeling between me and whomever I'm talking to. But, at the university, where I am trying to develop my thinking, I sense I am often insensitive—too quick and uncaring about what the other person has to say, too anxious to put my views over. The trouble is that this part of me is like a thoroughbred horse that needs exercising—there is no other time/opportunity for me to express myself, except in seminars or lectures. If I "hold my horses" they never would get exercise. But there is this overwhelming element which I sense and dislike in myself. I don't know what to do about it. Home is super—children happy and fun—so why can't I accept Brunel for what it is? Take what is good and ignore what is not. This continual irritation and moaning about its rottenness is pure animus. The Buddha says, "See the world as it is—not as you would like it to be." Said to me by a strange man at a party on Saturday—it hits the nail on head about Brunel.

Jung's theory of psychological types explained why I was insensitive to people. I first heard about Jung's theory from a lecture at the Jung club before I started analysis and I was fascinated by it, initially because I thought it would explain my mother's antagonism towards me. Did she dislike me, I wondered, because I was a different type to her? But soon I left that question behind and became intrigued by the theory of psychological types and how it related to my own development.

Jung's classification of introvert and extrovert is generally accepted now by psychologists and his theory of types has been expanded and disseminated very successfully by Myers-Briggs. For me, the theory of personality types was not an academic exercise. It excited me because it explained to me so much about myself and about other people. There are four psychological types: thinking, feeling, sensation, and intuition. Each person has a dominant function; this is what they feel confident in and how they operate in the world. But each person also has an inferior function in which they feel less confident. It often trips them up and makes them anxious.

I began to see that I was an intuitive/thinking type. This meant that once I had started to develop my thinking, it felt natural and easy for me. Intuition was very useful to me as a therapist—I could sense the possibilities in people, pick up nuances and sense what was going on. But there was also a negative side to intuition—it could make me manipulative because I could sense how things ought to be and consequently would try to make them go that way.

I found the concept of the inferior function fascinating. In many cases, it was easier to spot a person's type by looking at what they were bad at, rather than what they were good at. Sensation/feeling are my inferior functions. The word sensation, in this context, is confusing. It is a translation of the German word *Gefühl*. Myers-Briggs translates the word as sensing, which to me is equally inexplicable. Sensation means down-to-earth practical stuff. Sensation types understand mechanics; they can put things together and take them apart, they are good at handling money, making holiday arrangements, and mending the washing machine. They see the nitty gritty but not the whole picture. I am the opposite. I see the whole picture and I am not good at focusing on detail. For me, mechanical, practical, and technical things make me anxious. This is because they relate to my inferior sensation function. My feeling function is also inferior; my emotions and feelings are often raw and uncontrollable. Also, in the past, though maybe less so now, I was often insensitive to other people, though this was never intentional.

When I first became aware of the theory of types, I realised that using my inferior functions made me feel unconfident and out of control, as if I was in a foreign country. But I found using them was also exhilarating and, in many ways, liberating. For instance, when I had mended the lawnmower, which took ages, I had a wonderful feeling of achievement. When I started to handle the family finances, as I will relate later on, though terrifying at first, this brought a considerable feeling of fulfilment.

Many parts of the course at Brunel did not interest me. One of the first essays we were asked to write at the beginning of the course was 'Is psychology an art or a science?' For me, without doubt, it was an art. But as the course progressed, it became increasingly clear to me that academic psychology was predominantly a science. It seemed to me that psychology at the university was trying to emulate other scientific disciplines in order to achieve respectability. I had done very little science at school, I didn't understand this approach, and it did not appeal to me. But I wanted to get a degree and therefore I had to conform to the university's requirements.

Every student in the psychology department had to devise an experiment. We were put into groups of three. I was put in a group with two young students, Estelle and Frankie. I didn't really understand what an experiment involved, and I was very reluctant to spend time doing it. I preferred to spend my time working on essays at home. Frankie and Estelle seemed as lost as I was and at our first meeting none of us had the slightest idea of what sort of experiment we wanted to do.

Pondering this problem that evening at home, I realised the way to make the project interesting for me was to incorporate Jung into it. He had a scientific background and at the beginning of his career had used association tests to demonstrate the existence of complexes. The following day, I suggested to Frankie and Estelle that we use association tests for our experiment, and they were happy to go along with this. They didn't really care what the experiment was, as long as they got a good mark towards their degrees. Michael, the lecturer in charge of the module, said that using association tests would be acceptable.

In association tests, subjects are read a list of words to which they are asked to respond with the first word that comes to mind. For instance, if the word read to them is 'swan' the response might be 'bird'. The reaction time to each word is recorded by a Galvanic Skin Response (GSR) machine. Jung's seminal research showed that words that had an emotional connotation would have a longer reaction time. This delayed reaction time suggested a complex—an unconscious psychic wound. In this way, Jung demonstrated that unconscious factors can influence conscious functioning.

I didn't anticipate that every step of the process would be fraught with problems and each procedure would take far longer than I expected.

JOURNAL (January 1978) Vicissitudes of an experiment. We put the idea of using association tests to Michael Wright, the lecturer in charge of the module. He introduces us to Harry, one of the technicians. Harry shows us how to use the GSR machine. Says only knob we should touch is central one. I ask him if I can look at test library to get a standardise version of association tests. He says only Helen and Lynda have the key.

I hang around in the corridor of the psychology department for most of the afternoon hoping to find one or the other. Then somebody tells me that Lynda has flu. So I wait outside Helen's room, hoping that she is still at the university. When eventually she turns up, I have to wait while she makes a couple of phone calls. She then tells me that she hasn't a key to the test library. Her secretary, Pamela, has it, but she was at a meeting at present. Helen says she will leave a note for Pamela. Very frustrated, I go home, having wasted an afternoon and achieved nothing.

As soon as I get back to university the next day, I go to find Pamela. She is very helpful and opens the door to the test library. To my dismay, it is a chaotic mess, boxes of files piled on top of each other. The filing cabinets dotted around the room are all locked. There is no catalogue. How on earth am I going to find association tests among this mess? The next day, I catch Helen between lectures, and she opens the door to the library—but she hasn't a key for the large filing cupboard in which she says the tests are probably kept.

I track down Frankie and Estelle in the students union bar, and tell them that I haven't been able to find a standardised test. I say to them we will have to concoct our own. I also say that we need to decide what our experiment will be. For our methodology, we have agreed that we will use association tests but what is the hypothesis that we want to test? Estelle and Frankie are even more clueless than me and also completely lacking in any initiative. I realise that if we were going to get this experiment off the ground, I will have to do the majority of the work. Frankie and Estelle are willing to help but they are not interested in the project and are happy to leave all the organisation to me.

We start to do the experiment by testing ourselves and find the GSR machine doesn't work and that Harry has had to go to London for an unspecified period. Another technician, Mark, says he doesn't understand the machine, but will see if he can find instructions.

Michael then comes on the scene and spends hours (literally) trying to get the GSR machine to work. Eventually he scrubs one machine and installs another—a Russian model which has to be filled with red ink by a hypodermic needle. Sometimes it works, sometimes it doesn't—frequently one of the contacts doesn't operate. Frankie and Estelle try out the GSR on various subjects with mixed success. We are shown again how to operate the dials and calibrate the machine. This time we are told on no account to touch the central knob, but we can alter all the others.

We decide that a man's voice is probably best for the experiment. We ask a friend of Estelle's to record a list of words onto a tape—but find there is too much background noise on the cassette. Mark, the technician, says he will do it for us. We give him four separate lists of words for the four tests. Because we are running so far behind on the experiment, Michael says we can divide it into two.

On Friday, Estelle brings a subject up to the room where we have set up the GSR machine, but, to our dismay, find Mark has not had time to record a cassette with the test words. We search the building for a man and find a first-year student in the common room who agrees to record this for us. When he has done so, we discover that the mike is not working and no recording has been made. By the time the technician has sorted this out, the student has to leave for a lecture. By this time we have two subjects we have enlisted, waiting to be tested. We look for another man—and the whole building seems deserted except for rather imposing men whom I don't dare approach. Estelle is braver than me and after four unsuccessful attempts, gets a man who records the list for us.

At last, we seat our subject in the chair and start the test—to find that the timing device isn't working—it either won't start or won't stop. The technician comes to mend it. By the time he has done this, both our subjects have to leave to attend seminars. Total time this morning three hours and nothing achieved.

In the following months, I began to realise that there was no point in complaining about the inadequacies of Brunel, that as a student I could do nothing to change the place; instead, I needed to harness the animus energy to my work. I knew that as I gained in confidence, the less the animus would take over. But how, I wondered, could I assimilate his power with my newly developed thinking? I was learning to think clearly and decisively but it was a new area for me, and I didn't feel confident in it, although I was learning to be less abrasive and more tactful.

JOURNAL (March 1980) An encounter with John Odling Smee today which set me thinking. He is a very bright, enthusiastic and powerful lecturer on evolutionary theory. Today we discussed a paper he has written. I had spent all morning working on it, so was not out of my depth. However, after about twenty minutes of the seminar, he asked a question to which I replied and he said very abruptly, "Wrong!" and turned to someone else and the discussion continued. I was shaken by this because I didn't think I was wrong and as the seminar continued, I could see that what I said was perfectly valid—he was saying just the same thing but using different words. It happened several times more (chiefly to me, but not exclusively) and at the end of the seminar, John said we obviously did not understand his paper. I then said that it seemed as if he was misunderstanding us. I didn't think we had misunderstood him. He made a friendly comment about communication being like a Pinter play, and we all left in a friendly mood. Afterwards, two members of the seminar said to me that they agreed with me—he was misunderstanding us—and I said I thought he was probably tired—it being near the end of term.

At the end of my third year at Brunel, I made an appointment to see my tutor, Michael Wright, to ask him why I wasn't getting As for my essays.

"What's wrong with my work?" I asked. To my delight, Michael gave me an answer which hit the nail on the head.

"You answer the questions correctly, you give all the right references and your essays are perfectly adequate. That's why you get B+. If you want to get A, you have to think originally, you have to start thinking critically about the issues, not just following the established guidelines."

And then he added, "Basically, what your work is missing is curiosity."

I found his comments extraordinarily helpful and exciting. How I wish I had asked his advice at the beginning of the course! Michael's comments have stayed with me and influenced everything I have done subsequently.

PSYCHIATRY

THE COURSE AT Brunel University was unusual in that it was a split course. For six months each year, students worked in a job in the community. I was placed in a huge psychiatric hospital in the west of London, which had existed since Victorian times. The hospital was like a village. It had a church, laundry, playing fields, industrial units; portacabins for art therapy, music therapy, and consultants' offices scattered around the grounds. Stick-like figures with a strange gait were walking around; these were patients—some of whom I got to know—who had lived there all their adult life. The strange walk was caused by their medication.

My placement was in the psychology department, run by an elderly Hungarian called Eva Martin. Heaven knows why she agreed to take on a student, because she did not know what to do with me. She didn't feel confident enough about me to let me see any patients, and sometimes exploded with anxiety when she did not know what I was up to.

JOURNAL (April 1978) What a place! Eva in the most terribly overwrought anxious state, looking as if she hasn't slept all weekend, shouting at me reams of stuff about me not doing this, that and the other. I wish I knew what had upset her—I have arranged a long session with her tomorrow. Someone has been getting at her, I guess, saying Virginia has not got enough to do— or something like this. I shall have to try and keep calm tomorrow and soothe her and sort things out.

Because I was given nothing to do, I wandered around the hospital exploring the different units—addiction unit, music therapy, art therapy, the day hospital—and talked to as many people as I could, hoping somebody would give me something to do. I came to realise that I had been placed in the wrong department. The psychology department was very suspicious of psychotherapy. To them I was a threat and worry—was I a therapist or a first-year student? If it was the first, they didn't want me around, if the second they didn't want me either as I didn't know anything. It was strange for me to feel depressed at work but that is how being at the hospital made me feel in those early months. If I did find something to do, I was in trouble with the psychology department because this made them anxious. If I didn't have anything to do, I felt bored and aimless. It was often a relief to leave the hospital at the end of the day to go home to the hurly-burly of family life.

Belinda and Alexander were engaging children; their interactions and conversations kept me endlessly amused. Alexander was a very intelligent little boy, determined to keep up with the others. He had a dream which he recounted with gusto one morning at breakfast. "I go to Switzerland on holiday (I was meant to go to America but this man in CID wanted me to go to help him.) When I am there, some bank robbers hold up a bank. They say to me, 'Hand over all your money.' I have money in one pocket, but in the other I have a gun. (I am a secret agent and always carry a gun.) I pretend to look for money and pull out my gun and capture the robbers. I do this ten times and each time I get a large reward—£50—so I get £500 altogether."

Ever since this dream, Alexander stopped being frightened of witches and baddies; he could now go upstairs by himself and did not put a chair against the cupboard door when he went to bed. Altogether he became more confident. A few days later, when he came home from school on the bus by himself, he was not put out to find fares had gone up and he did not have enough money.

JOURNAL (June 1978) After half term holiday. Odd coming back after ten days break from the hospital. I've forgotten the insecurity and aimlessness of having no job—also I had under-estimated the anxiety in the psychology department. I am back to the old game of trying to find something to do without upsetting anybody—torn between total inactivity and boredom, and activity which makes psychology staff insecure.

Worst bit of day was overhearing, in the Day Hospital, Freda, the social worker, talk to a very disturbed girl, Jocelyn, who is being admitted to Ellis ward. She obviously has a long history of schizo-phrenia and has inflicted injury to herself—but she is intelligent, and what she can't bear, reasonably, is been parted from her 17-month-old daughter. Freda was arrogant and punitive—awful. "All parents have to learn to cope with anxiety," she said in her superior voice.

Half an hour session with Eva this afternoon. Impossible to be cross with her or even ask anything from her—because she is very well-meaning and anxious—one has just to listen and soothe. As I sat with her today, I wondered what it would feel like to be a patient—I think she would make me feel inadequate and anxious! Anyway, she seems satisfied with what I am doing but is not able to put anything in my way. She is happy for me to work it out for myself as long as she knows what I am doing—I have to log it in a huge diary—rather irritating to have to be accountable!

After six weeks, I went to see my tutor, Michael Wright, at Brunel. He was reassuring and helpful.

JOURNAL (June 1978) Michael said to me he used to work under someone like Eva so knows what it is like. He was sorry I was in this situation but said that I was there to learn something, that such things have a purpose, and I've got to learn how to make use of it. Such a wise comment! He helped me to see that one learns much more from difficult situations and from making mistakes—and that is what I am doing all the time at the moment!

After two months of wandering around the hospital looking for something to do, I met a psychiatrist who, to my delight and astonishment, offered me what I had been expecting when I initially joined the hospital. Dr B was willing to let me interview patients, attend his outpatient clinics, attend his ward rounds, and go with him on home visits. At last I was doing what I wanted to do. From then on, the hospital became an exciting place to be. Eva Martin became increasingly agitated by my disappearance from her waiting room, so I asked Dr B if he would be my supervisor and he was happy to do this. Eva was very relieved to see me go.

Dr B was an unusual man. He was a psychoanalyst as well as consultant psychiatrist, about 60, quite small, with a charming smile and a German accent. Like many small men, he liked being in a position of power, and I thought this was why he was so kind to me: he was my patron. There were other members of his entourage who had a similar relationship to him, people who didn't have the right qualifications for the jobs they were doing. They were often very good at what they did, but it meant they were obligated to him.

At the beginning, Dr B's referrals to me were mostly in-patients who had been in the hospital for years; one or two were in locked wards. For me, it was engrossing and fascinating, getting to know these very tragic figures who usually were delighted to talk to someone who was interested in them. Two patients from that time I remember particularly. They were both in locked wards. When I arrived, I rang a bell and a nurse came to open the door with a bunch of keys hanging from his belt. This was a male ward, and all the nurses were male and were very suspicious of me. I tried to talk to them about the patients, but they distrusted me and thought my contact with their patients was disruptive and harmful.

Tim, who had been in hospital since he was 18, was a good-looking, gentle man in his late twenties. His diagnosis was schizophrenia, but I couldn't discover why he was in a locked ward. He didn't want to talk about why he was there, and he never mentioned hallucinations or hearing voices. Our meetings were very pleasant, but the content felt inconsequential—until one day he told me he felt bottled up and longed to express his feelings. He said he would like to scream and shout.

I asked the charge nurse if we could use the padded cell for our next session. The cell had no furniture, no windows, and the walls were covered in soft material. There was a small window in the door, and I saw a nurse looking through every now and then. Tim and I sat on the floor. He seemed very tense and uncomfortable. This was not his accustomed milieu. I explained that he could shout and scream as much as he liked—this was what the room was for. He looked at me like an animal in pain; I could see it in his eyes, but all he could do was sit on the ground, immobile, with his arms around his knees. Tim and I tried the padded cell for two sessions and then returned to the corner of the day room on the ward where we had talked when I first met him. He was always pleased to see me and greeted me with a smile, but I didn't feel I made any progress with him whatsoever.

David was a different proposition. He was a dark, bearded man who had been on Blair Ward, another locked ward, for the past year. He strongly objected to being there and had applied to the mental health tribunal for his release. David opened up a lot to me. He told me he had been diagnosed as paranoid schizophrenic because he had attacked his mother, but he explained that this was because she was an infuriating woman. He didn't see why, just because he had lost his temper, he should be shut up in a psychiatric hospital. I tended to agree with him. At that stage, I was always on the patient's side.

JOURNAL (July 1978) This morning, I attended Blair ward round at which we discussed David and I found myself in very deep water. The fact that he is appealing to the mental health tribunal makes members of staff feel very defensive and anxious—they feel they are being criticised for not doing their job properly. I said how I was finding David (unsociable, solitary, hermit-like, but not a danger to anyone). The Charge Nurse disagreed—said David's brother and mother had told him of violence also of most bizarre behaviour, though there was no evidence of this on the ward. The ward round was particularly tense because David's brother and sister-in-law had come to see Dr B without an appointment and were waiting outside to see him. Difficult situation for me of divided loyalties—I tried to make my peace afterwards with Dr Cruikshank, the junior doctor, and will go and have a chat with the Charge Nurse on Friday. It is important they don't feel I am undermining them.

After the ward round, I spent half an hour with David—it was difficult because builders were making a racket outside and we had to shout at each other above the din. He is adamant that the hospital can't help him, that he is going ahead with his appeal, that he won't work at the ITU (Industrial Training Unit) for £7 per week—and although I tried to show him the other side, my heart wasn't in it—because I'm not convinced that hospital can help him. The only thing that I feel very unsure about is his home situation. What is he like at home? What is his mother like? Without knowing that, it is not possible to come down definitely either way. But on the evidence presented to me, it seems wrong that he should be kept forcibly in hospital.

It is a pity that our sessions will end at the end of September when term begins again at Brunel as we have a good working relationship and I think it helps him. He is adamant about the tribunal and is refusing to work at the ITU. Today he told the Charge Nurse he didn't trust him further than he could kick him, but otherwise he is behaving well. He thinks staff have it in for him because of the appeal—they wouldn't let him go to bed at 8 p.m. yesterday although he had previously. For the first time, we talked about schizophrenia.

Later on, when I had more experience of working in psychiatry, I saw a wider picture and recognised that the diagnosis of paranoid schizophrenia is not made arbitrarily but is very carefully considered and based on a worldwide classification. At that time, I didn't feel confident enough to raise this with Dr B, who had made the diagnosis. David lost his appeal to the mental health tribunal and afterwards refused to see me.

As he gained confidence in my ability, Dr B gave me lots of referrals, patients from his outpatient clinics, and also patients we saw together on home visits. At last I felt I was using my therapeutic skills. I was also learning a great deal about psychiatry. I met Dr B in my first year's work placement and each subsequent year I went back to work in his team at the hospital and, as he and his team got to know me and trust me, I was given more work with in-patients and out-patients.

Shirley, who had been on Avon ward for two years, taught me a lot about obsessive compulsive behaviour. She was 30 and, for as long as she could remember, she had been tortured by irrational fears. These she tried to control by doing rituals. She was a pleasant woman, very open and easy to talk to, and after our first session, I felt optimistic I could help her. She seemed capable of taking things in, was dissatisfied with her life, and wanted to get better. She said that her life was a mess and wanted to do something about it. A student social worker called Pat had tried to help her the previous year, and Shirley had enjoyed her sessions with her. Pat was much the same age as me and quite like me, Shirley said, so she was able to carry on with me where she had left off with Pat.

Shirley had two voices. The first voice was a normal voice in which she answered questions about herself and she described her life to me. The second voice, which would interrupt the first, was a sort of sing-song voice in which described her actions. "Open bag, take out handkerchief, that's it," or "Stand up, open door, that's it," or "look down corridor, check no one is there, that's it." It seemed that the second sing-song voice was the only way she could operate without being overwhelmed by her phobias. She was fearful of taking any action—even going to the toilet was a problem for her. She often wet the bed at night and, most times that I saw her, she had wet jeans. It was as if her ego was absent; there was no one in charge of her personality. She was unable to take control of her actions and she was dominated by fears.

My optimism about Shirley was misplaced. I learned that she wasn't capable of changing. She did not have the ego strength to stand up to her fears. She was always very pleased to see me and always pleasant to talk to, but she remained tortured by her fears and obsessions. I realised with sadness that the only way to help Shirley live a normal life was through the support of medication.

Another patient I felt very optimistic about at the beginning was Beatrice, also an in-patient on Avon ward. Beatrice was a singer, who had been diagnosed as schizophrenic. Before she became ill, she'd had an interesting career as a member of the BBC singers. Her first breakdown had happened while she was preparing for a solo recital at the Wigmore Hall in 1974. She had a devoted husband, Derek, who visited her every day and filled me in about her career.

I started to see Beatrice twice a week and was thrilled by her progress. As she talked about herself, she seemed to come to life, and lost the apathetic demeanour of a psychiatric patient. A lively, intelligent woman started to emerge. This thrilled me, as it did her husband. The ward staff were amazed. Could Beatrice really emerge from her psychotic state and become a normal person again? This appeared to be the case. After a few weeks, the staff were happy for her to be discharged from the ward and she started to live at home again. Derek took leave from work to be with her and brought her to the outpatient clinic twice a week for her sessions with me. Everything went well for several weeks until Derek had to go back to work. He arranged for a neighbour to be with Beatrice every day but this was not enough support for her. A week later, at her session, I was dismayed to find she had regressed. The psychotic stare in her eyes had returned. She was limp, like a rag doll. I tried to get through to her, to help her to see how essential Derek was to her well-being, but her ability to engage with me and work on herself had gone. With great sadness, I saw Beatrice return to being an in-patient on the ward. I continued to see her until the term began again at Brunel. She was put back onto antipsychotic medication and, when I saw her last, she had reverted to being an apathetic psychiatric patient.

When I was at work, I often felt anxious about the younger children—an anxiety that most working mothers will recognise. Francis was working at home in his studio in the garden and I knew he would cope with an emergency. But he could not be asked to look after the children. By the time Tina and Simon had left home, Belinda and Alexander were old enough to look after themselves, but in those early years I relied on the big children to look after the little ones. One day when I came home, I was greeted with great excitement.

"Tina has a boyfriend!" shouted Alexander. William had spotted Tina at the bus stop as she waited to go to school. He had asked her to go to a film that evening. The little children were beside themselves with excitement. Tina, a very attractive 16-year-old, wondered what all the fuss was about, but I noticed that she took a lot of trouble about her appearance before she went out that evening.

Those four years, when I spent six months each year at the psychiatric hospital, were an invaluable training in psychiatry. After meeting Dr B and seeing patients with him and on my own, I learnt about differential diagnoses, about medication and its side-effects, about the different therapies available, and the relationship between the different disciplines in the hospital. It was often depressing to see how little help was available for psychiatric patients and how little had changed in treatment for fifty years. The only new development appeared to be the introduction in the 1950s of phenothiazines to treat psychotic illnesses. These drugs acted like a corset to control the symptoms. Unfortunately, they were often prescribed without caution and the patients were over medicated. What I learnt during those years provided the foundation for my subsequent work at Ashford hospital and in my private practice.

ON MY OWN

JOURNAL (March 1980) I can cope without Faye. I know how to do it (sort of) and I will try to do what Jung did and follow psyche's direction. It feels like being pushed out of the nursery, where I was safe and nurtured, into the world with very little protection. Protection from Nancy? Yes, that is my real fear, that without Faye, I will be vulnerable to my mother's attacks and fall back into the old pattern of behaviour.

WHEN FAYE BECAME ill and stopped working, I felt adrift, alone, and unsupported. I also felt vulnerable and unable to defend myself against my mother's attacks. Usually, these were on the telephone. She would say things that hit me below the belt and upset me for days afterwards. My friends said I had a phobia about the telephone because often I didn't answer it. But this was because I dreaded phone calls from my mother.

Here is an example of one of her attacks. At Christmas, we often went to my sister's house in Andover where Christmas lunch was done with great style. One year, I offered to do the Christmas lunch at our house in Chiswick for my sister's family, my family and my mother. We would be thirteen altogether. It was a huge under-taking because I had to do everything—the shopping, the cooking, the presents, laying the table, decorating the tree. Afterwards, I felt exhausted but satisfied with how it had gone; there had been enough food, it had tasted good, and everybody had a good time.

The next day my mother phoned. I thought she would say, "That was a really nice lunch yesterday. We all enjoyed ourselves." But that is not what she said.

"Why are you so unkind to Juliet's children?" she asked. "Juliet was very upset by the way you behaved yesterday." I loved Juliet's children and I was not aware I had been unkind to them in any way. I was struck dumb; I didn't know how to reply to her criticism. For days afterwards I was torn with misery about it.

Now I understand why this happened. I was my mother's shadow, the negative part of her personality. If I did anything right, she had to turn it into something wrong; she had to see the negative in me. Otherwise, she would have had to own the negative in herself and this would have made her feel depressed. Everything that wasn't admirable about her personality, my mother projected onto me. I was the dustbin into which she put all the shitty side of herself. This pathological interaction suited Juliet. It was hard on her having a sister only a year younger, who was brighter and, as we grew older, prettier. It has taken me a long time to realise that Juliet, whom I loved and admired, relished my unhappiness and often contributed to it.

JOURNAL (January 1981) I am beginning to realise that the way to serenity—to wholeness—is to be at one with my unconscious self—that the panic and anxiety are the result of a split in me. My dreams are showing me very clearly the way to go. If I keep my mind on reconciling conscious with unconscious—then I am moving in the direction which is right for me. When my mind gets filled with worries and anxieties, that is when I get more and more tense. I am beginning to see that much of what I do is driven by the desire to please—and this is to compensate for my inner feeling of inadequacy. I feel I have to please to make up for being a bad girl. When I can feel my adequacy and wholeness, I won't any longer be driven by the desire to please. I also realise that what is mine may be small and insignificant—what matters is that it is mine—it comes from my centre—by which I mean, not from ego but from Self. The ego is showing Nancy I am as good as Adam and Juliet. The Self is doing what is right and natural for me.

There is a happy ending to my relationship with my mother. In her late 80s, she had a series of ministrokes and lost her memory. But, although she was not the vibrant, charismatic character she had been in the past, she was still able to function very well. The miraculous part for me was that she "forgot" to be critical of me. She became a sweet old lady whose company I enjoyed, and she was always pleased to see me. From then, until her death six years later, I had a loving relationship with my mother, such as I had always hoped for.

Shortly after Faye stopped working, my inner life began to change. As I worked on my own, I found that my frustration at being stuck and not digging deeper fell away. My dreams became acute and relevant. I gained new insights—I felt in charge of my own process. Faye had taught me how to work with dreams, but while I was with her they remained trivial and inconsequential. Without her, my dreams developed urgency and movement. I didn't put the two together immediately—the sterility of the dreams while I was seeing Faye and the vibrancy when I was on my own. But, as I worked on the dreams, I began to see the sickness in our relationship, and realise that Faye should never have taken me on for analysis.

Trying to see a pattern
To make sense
Of buffeting emotions
The turbulence in my life
Ingredients, raw materials
Into the melting pot
Keeping the lid on
By holding down the lid
Not dissipating the process
Not talking about it
Trivialising it
Diluting it.

During this time, as I worked at understanding myself, I often felt very shaken and unconfident as I questioned everything. I felt as if I was taking myself apart and I was in pieces. Feelings of inferiority seemed intertwined with everything. Was there anything true in my personality, I wondered. Was there anything that came from the Self? I hung onto the belief that the centre of me was real and true, but it had been distorted because of my inferiority/superiority complex.

As I worked on this, I felt I was coming down to earth, and I began to see a pattern. I realised that when things were difficult, I escaped into the clouds as a defence against pain. This pattern of behaviour had started when I was emerging from childhood. Then, I often felt despairing about myself. But, to survive, I repressed the despair and escaped into a cloud of superiority. Being Jewish, belonging to the church, being married to a musician, the jobs I did, having a large family—all of these I would point to as evidence of my superiority. When Ben died, I followed the same pattern of behaviour. It was unbearable to accept the tragedy. I repressed the feelings of being a bad mother. I became more and more manic in my determination to be special, superior to everyone else. I said to the world I can cope with anything. Eventually my body, illness—myxoedema—brought me down to earth. And then I had the visions. Although the vibrancy of the visions stayed with me, I didn't understand them.

JOURNAL (March 1980) It seems that every time I crash, I have the opposite and then swing into that. When I was ill, I had the visions and they made me feel very special. I put my faith in them 100 per cent, but when I couldn't enact them, I crashed again. Bloody hell! It's been the same problem, over and over again— and each time I have failed to solve it. Either I am up in the clouds, or I am stuck in depression. The confusion of special complex with Self—swinging from manic above it all to depressive stuck position.

What I need to do is separate the two and hold both positions i.e. holding the opposites—maintaining a mid-position. Accepting my ordinary, human self, but at the same time acknowledging the divine Self. I am an ordinary woman—but there is a divine thread running through my life, a divine centre, as there is with all of us. I have been aware of it—I've identified with it or rejected it. Now I must get the relationship right. It feels extraordinarily painful coming down to earth, without letting go of the vision. It feels intolerable and impossible. Great feeling of pain inside. No, no, no, I can't bear this—I will lose everything—I shall be lost—it's not safe—I'm exposed. I can't bear to be so unprotected; it feels an impossible position. How can I hold the two together? Not lose hold of the vision—but keep my feet firmly on the ground. It makes me feel as if I'm going to burst.

My mother rang to tell me that Faye had died when I was in the middle of exams at Brunel. I had to put it out of my mind until they were over. Then I felt overwhelmed with sadness about her death. The world seemed a bleak place without her. I longed to see her again to thank her for getting me going and to tell her how my inner analyst was helping me surge forward in my individuation.

The week after Faye died, I was in a very emotional state; it was a week unlike any I had known before. I began to understand things I hadn't before. Synchronistic events kept on happening; everything in my life seemed to be covered in a glorious cloak of relevance. Looking back, I can see that at that time I was dipping in and out of the unconscious and that is why my perception was so acute.

A few weeks later, I was sitting in my study at home, in one of the armchairs - the other, for patients, was empty. I was alone, thinking about Faye. Then it was as if I saw Faye—really saw her or imagined her, I'm not sure—but she was a vibrant presence. She was standing by the chair opposite me, and I had the sense that there was something she wanted me to do. But what?

Over the coming weeks, I would puzzle about this. I encouraged the Analytical Psychology Club to set up a memorial lecture series named the Faye Pye lectures. I went to see Arnold, her husband, and he kindly gave one of her books, Hannah Arendt's *The Human Condition*. I dreamt that I met Faye and showed her the book Arnold had given me and she was irritated, as if I had misunderstood her. What did Faye want me to do?

JOURNAL (June 1980) Today, I was reading a bit of "Memories" where Jung describes a dream he had a year after his wife's death, in which she was continuing to work on the Grail legend. He says it seems to him that after death people continue to work at their individuation, to finish what they had to do. As I read this, I found myself crying about Faye—and thinking about her unfinished work.

I tried to put the nagging discontent out of my mind, but the pressure remained; there was something I had to do—that Faye wanted me to do. In August, after eight months of working on my own, I decided I had to get a new analyst if I wanted to enter the AJA training scheme. Of all the Jungian analysts in London (there are not many of the Zurich group) the only one who did not know my mother was Sasha Duddington, so I decided to contact him. The strange thing was, that as I dialled his number and he answered, I felt Faye's relief. At last I had done what she was urging me to do. From that moment, she went away—and became a figure in the past—no longer influencing my life.

SASHA

JOURNAL (August 1980) I think it will be OK with Duddington—he is introverted feeling intuitive—not very articulate, but a very kind shy quality about him and an integrity which I like. I also like his cosy little study up in the roof, overlooking the heath—with family noise about—so much more congenial and real than a sterile consulting room.

I WENT TO see Sasha Duddington at the beginning of August 1980 and arranged to start analysis with him in September. In the intervening four weeks until I saw him again, I was left feeling very churned up. Was I right to go to see him? What does he think of me? Have I misrepresented myself? Have I misrepresented Faye? Round and round went these questions. But I also wondered, Why was I going on like this? Why was I upset? Why couldn't I put it away until I saw him at the end of the month? I came to realise that these questions remained in my head, continually bugging me, because there was something I needed to sort out.

First, I didn't want to use Sasha as a bucket. I didn't want to talk at him, off-load onto him. I wanted to be able to relate to him.

Relating to patients was not a problem for me. But when I was the patient, I felt very vulnerable and tended to escape into myself and forget about the other person. I tended to use them as a bucket. In mulling over what I wanted to say to Sasha, I knew I had to learn to relate to him through feeling, but I didn't know how to do this. I told myself I didn't need to impress him, that it didn't matter if he misjudged me because whatever happened, my golden centre was there—and I could only be in touch with that and with him by staying with feeling—offering my inferior side. "Forget what I'm good at—that can look after itself," I told myself. I knew that if I wanted to be in touch with the Self, then I had to let go of my sure ground and venture into the sea—like St Peter walking on water.

Second, two complexes had been activated by going to see Sasha: the need to be special and the fear of being misunderstood. The special complex had dogged me all my life—*I'm special, I'm entitled, I'm better than other people.* When I started to examine my own pathology, it was easy to see that this complex originated in childhood. Then I was made to feel bad, second class, unworthy, unlikable, inferior to my brother and sister, and to my mother, who was very special—everybody loved her, everybody admired her. In the analysis with Faye, the special complex was often discussed. Why did I need to feel special? Faye never traced it back to childhood; she used to get on her high horse and say how people today feel so anonymous, they need to stand out and be acknowledged. After Faye, my struggles with the special complex continued. I knew I wasn't superior to other people; I also knew I wasn't inferior. But how to get it right, how to achieve the balance between superior and inferior?

JOURNAL (September 1980) I consulted the *I Ching* to find out if I've done the right thing in going to see Duddington, as it has left me feeling quite churned up and uncertain. I got a hexagram which speaks straight to me:

Deliverance
Return brings good fortune.
Hastening brings good fortune
Thunder and pain get in.
The image of deliverance.
Thus the superior man pardons mistakes and forgives misdeeds. . .
In life this brings a release from tensions similar to that produced
in nature
By the cleansing of the air after a thunderstorm.
If there are any residual matters that ought to be attended to,
It should be done as quickly as possible
So that a clean sweep is made and no retardations occur.

This hexagram says to me that I was right to go to see Sasha and tell him what I did about Faye—the atmosphere has got to be cleared and tension released. I had to show him where I am.

Sasha was a small, shy, bald-headed man. I felt immediately at home with him. After my first session with him, telling him about Faye and my mother, I felt great relief and a feeling of peace. It seemed to me that everything was falling into place. This was, I thought, because I was taking a back seat—just letting things happen, not manipulating or controlling them.

Several private patients were referred to me by Dr B and I turned the small sitting room in the front of the house into a consulting room. It was ideally situated by the front door.

JOURNAL (October 1980) My poor ego still worries and fusses and finds it exceedingly difficult to let go and let things happen. Years of habitually taking control are not easy to unlearn. Brunel brings it out very much and so does my natural anxiety about getting the new patients going. But I'm working at just letting things happen—not pushing, not seeking, but being receptive to whatever happens, knowing that there is an underlying pattern. I hope I will never lose this feeling of centredness, this inner contentment.

Seeing patients at home was an important milestone for me: it represented my work being recognised by my family (particularly Francis) and I felt much more loving and receptive to him as a result. In the past, I felt that he was shutting out this valuable part of me.

There was a warm, joyous feeling about analysing with Sasha. He met me where I was, he let me just be myself; we were able to discuss a drawing, or a dream, and he was able to understand what it was about and to give me a feeling of support and stability.

JOURNAL (October 1980) Today I made a whole series of drawings—which have helped me enormously. First a series of mandalas—then a drawing of the collective unconscious like an enormous Persian carpet and my little eye glimpsing a minute part of it. This one scared me. And then I felt reassured by another, which showed my golden centre in a womb-like object—like me, wounded, not perfect—but the centre is not affected by what it is contained in. Then there was a drawing of four sunflowers growing from a snake.

I used to drive across London to Hampstead twice a week. Sometimes I would arrive early and walk on the heath. It seemed very appropriate that Sasha's address was the Vale of Health. His small consulting room was on the top floor of the house. He would sit opposite me, notebook on his knee, pen in hand, his half-moon glasses perched on his nose. He looked like a bird. He would probe and ask questions but rarely made a comment. He was a shadowy figure and yet a reassuring presence.

Three weeks after I had started working with him, I took this dream to the session:

DREAM (October 12 1980) I am with Dr B at the hospital. It's all very friendly. I'm happy to be with him. Then there is a nurse standing by me.

He says to her: "I know your face, don't I?"

She says, "No, Dr B."

"Are you sure?"

In a coquettish way, she tugs at his shirt and then he remembers.

I feel embarrassed at being there as obviously something amorous took place between them. He goes off with the nurse, supposedly to find something for her. He comes back a few minutes later to collect the ladder from the porter.

I'd had several dreams previously about Dr B; most of them made me feel uncomfortable and I interpreted them to myself as an unresolved infantile part of me. This is the first one I took to Sasha.

"Who is the nurse?" Sasha asked. "And why are you embarrassed?"

As he probed the content of the dream, torrents of emotion overwhelmed me. I couldn't understand what was happening. Why was I upset? Why couldn't I stop shaking? Why was I on the verge of crying? Why was Dr B, that crusty old psychiatrist, causing these feelings in me to erupt?

Very gently, Sasha helped me to understand the dream: the nurse is Dr B's anima. I am embarrassed because I am out of touch with my anima qualities. The ladder symbolises development, his and mine. Over the next few days, I began to see that the dream was pushing me to recognise that through a relationship with Dr B I would discover my anima qualities, part of me which had laid dormant all my adult life.

The prospect of a relationship with Dr B terrified me. I didn't know how to do it, I didn't want to mess up my new career of which he was an important patron, and foremost was the fear that such a relationship could harm my marriage. It left me in a state of turmoil. I couldn't sleep. I felt as if I was living on two different levels, sleepwalking through life with this huge dilemma on my mind. I wanted to follow the path of individuation, I wanted to obey the promptings of psyche as shown in dreams. But here I was being asked to do something abhorrent—to form a relationship with a man whom I didn't find attractive and in doing so threaten the two most precious things in my life, my marriage, and my career. It terrified me.

Yet, strange as it may seem, I felt I had no option. I had made a commitment to psyche. I had committed myself to follow the promptings of my dreams wherever they took me. I was in a state of turmoil as this journal entry illustrates.

JOURNAL (October 1980) The pain of realising where the relationship with Dr B will lead me: that there can be no closed doors. I feel as if I am being torn apart. I can only relate to him by being open and receptive—and through the relationship with him, learn how to be a whole woman. The thought of letting go of Virginia is very painful—as Sasha says, the bride, the virgin, the unknowing one—to let that go and become a whole woman. I know now that is what the dream is saying to me—my embarrassment in the dream is the blockage in me. Ego is Virginia and I have got to let her go. Self is the path of individuation. It is miraculous to me that Sasha understands this and is travelling with me—guiding me, supporting me. The future has a feeling both of fear and of exhilaration about it—very unknown. There is also a feeling of expansion—of finding parts of myself I have never known.

For days, I was living in a mist. It was as if I had reached the top of a mountain but could not see the view. I could not see the context nor the difference between inner and outer. I could sense Sasha's concern but was just too tired to work on it. But as the mists cleared, I understood what Sasha meant by "you need a line to the land if you're going to plunge into the depths". At that time, I was not even aware that I had entered the unconscious. I could not see the difference between reality and unreality, between conscious and unconscious.

As I regained my equilibrium, I realised that I needed the down-to-earth stuff of Francis and the children. I told myself that without them I could end up like Nietzsche or any of the other characters who have ventured into the unknown territories of the psyche and become insane. Dr B was continually in my thoughts. I was turning over in my mind what I could say to him—thinking all the time about this man, an aching in my heart, a longing to be with him, wondering how to get through to him—a hurtful yearning not unlike how I used to feel about some patients on the ward rounds whom I felt I could help.

There was also this other part of me saying "Well really, Virginia! Are all your moral standards of so little substance that they can disintegrate because of a dream? You are planning to seduce a good, kind, respectable man—to entice him into a relationship with you." The thought horrified and frightened me. What was I doing? And yet the pain and longing continued. Was I kidding myself that psyche was pushing me to be Dr B's anima? I remembered the film with Jacques Tati as Don Camillo, a priest in a small village in Italy, arguing with Christ: "Really, Lord, you are being unreasonable—you don't realise what you are asking of me." This helped me a lot. I realised that this was what I was doing, baulking, resisting—I don't want to do this, and yet I was driven to do it.

When I first read the dream about Dr B and the nurse, it seemed inconsequential—just a dream, no particular meaning in it. But working on the dream with Sasha opened up torrents of feeling. It broke down barriers of a lifetime. It opened new horizons and it showed me the way forward. Working on that dream was one of the most momentous experiences of my life. Reading it again today, forty years later, my reaction is—what was all that about? There doesn't seem much there. But as I dwell on the images, it touches the old chord again and I begin to remember how I felt then and how terrifying were the implications of the dream. The anima part of me, the muse, the feminine, seductive, attractive, sexy girl, had been squashed and abandoned during all those years of marriage with Francis. She was an essential part of me—but to find her would mean upturning and threatening my marriage. It also threatened my security and my view of myself as a good girl, a moral girl with a rock-solid marriage.

I did not have a choice—I had decided, following Jung, to devote my life to psyche—to follow wherever it led, whatever the consequences. But it seemed it was forcing me to give up what I cherished most and put at risk my career in psychiatry, which was in its infancy. How could I start a relationship with Dr B? Did I want to? He was not attractive, a lot older than me, a crusty, inhibited, sad little man—yet my psyche was pushing me towards him, and I was unable to get him out of my head. I longed to be close to him, to help him, to show him the way forward. I was longing to be his anima.

Over and over in my mind, I pondered how to approach Dr B. I knew I had to tread very gently, and that, somehow, I had to get through to him in such a way that he did not feel threatened nor misinterpret what I was saying. Somehow, I had to share my feelings without inundating him. Also, I had to reassure him that there was room within our marriages for us to do our own thing: that there was a growing point between us for us to work on. How could I say this to him?

URY

I MADE AN appointment to see Dr B at the university where he held a clinic once a week for students. As I sat in the waiting room, among the other students, I was very scared. I hadn't slept all night. It seemed crazy what I was going to do. The whole situation seemed unreal.

Dr B was sitting, facing me, at a large desk with a window behind him.

"Well, Virginia," he said. "What can I do for you?"

"Dr B," I began tentatively, "I wondered if. . ."

There was a knock on the door and a secretary came into the room. "Sorry to disturb you, Dr B, could you sign these letters?" She stood by him as he signed the letters, a rather plump girl wearing a very short skirt. I felt a fleeting feeling of relief: was I being let off the hook? Was I being given the option to back out? But a deep feeling in my gut told me I had to say what I had prepared. As he signed the letters, I stared at a small brown birthmark on the back of the secretary's leg. Did she know it was there, I wondered? There were six letters for him to sign, he read each one, signed it and then handed it to the secretary. When she left the room, he smiled at me and said, "You were saying. . ."

I took a deep breath. "Dr B, I would like to have a relationship with you," I said, in a halting voice. I had been rehearsing what I wanted to say all night long, but as the words came out of my mouth, they sounded false, and I wanted to swallow them back. He looked at me in astonishment and dropped his pipe on the floor. There was an awkward silence.

"What do you have in mind?" he asked, as he bent down to pick up his pipe. I tried to explain and as I did so I could see the image of a frightened old woman. I knew I had to go very gently.

"I just wondered if we could get to know each other better," I said. "I could learn so much from you. I should love to learn more about psychiatry and the psychoanalytic approach."

To my amazement, he liked the idea and said, "Yes, let's explore this." He suggested we should meet for lunch the next day. I left his office in a dream. I couldn't believe I had done it and he had responded positively.

The next day we met in his portacabin in the hospital grounds; his secretary brought us sandwiches and coffee on a tray. He was very easy to talk to, he had a warm smile and I felt immediately at ease. We started talking about psychiatry and psychoanalytic theory, but very soon the focus was on him. I learnt that his real name was Ury, but when he came to England he used his second name, Bernard, which sounded more English. This is what his wife and his colleagues called him. He was very pleased when I said I would call him Ury.

As the weeks progressed, the relationship with Ury became an engrossing part of my life. In fact, I became obsessed by him. I could not get him out of my thoughts and found myself longing to be with him in a way I found intensely irritating. Who is this person who is longing to be with this old man, I wondered? Is it the adolescent bit of me or the unfulfilled middle-aged woman? When I took my worries to Sasha, he helped me to see that I was being driven by the myth of Pygmalion. In the Greek myth, Pygmalion is a sculptor who creates a stone statue and in doing so falls in love with the statue he has created.

JOURNAL (November 1980) The longing to be with Ury is pretty constant and also the throbbing feeling of life pulsing through me. Very strange, isn't it? When I don't even find him physically attractive. Yet it is this gripping feeling of coming to life that pervades my relationship with him. He is coming to life and me too; it's as if this is what I have to do.

A book that helped me greatly to understand what was happening to me was by Toni Wolff, Jung's associate. In *Structural Forms of the Feminine Psyche*, Wolff suggests that women's psyche has four aspects, all of which have to be developed to achieve wholeness. She calls the four aspects Mother, Hetaira, Amazon and Sophia. As with psychological types, one aspect is dominant and easy to develop, its opposite is in the shadow and is difficult to access and alien to consciousness. Mother is opposite to Hetaira, Sophia is opposite to Amazon.

Mother felt natural to me, I loved being a mother not only to my children but also to my patients. When Ben died, I lost confidence in being a mother, but after Belinda was born I regained this part of myself. Amazon—the career girl, the woman who can take her place in a man's world—was coming into consciousness with my degree at Brunel and the blossoming of my career. Hetaira—the girlfriend, the muse, sexual, attractive, seductive—had been around in my teens, but marriage to Francis had squashed her and she had disappeared into jeans, short hair and extra weight. At the beginning of the marriage, she was still bubbling at the surface but slowly over the years, she had shrivelled up, not died, but buried within me.

Hetaira frightened me. She threatened my image of myself as a loving wife and mother; although unconscious, she was very near the surface and often caused problems, getting me entangled with men without knowing how to handle it. It was a whole area of unconsciousness which was banging at the door to be made conscious. The dream of October 12, about Dr B and the nurse, had opened the floodgates. The thrust of individuation had pushed her up again, causing me at first embarrassment, but as she emerged into consciousness, she became a vibrant part of my personality.

The fourth aspect, Sophia, represents the wise woman. Now, in my old age, I may be getting glimmerings of what she is about. At this time of great turmoil in my life, Toni Wolff's book reassured me. It helped me to see what was happening—individuation was pushing me to develop the different aspects of my feminine personality.

I found Ury extremely congenial; he was as fascinated by psychology as I was. He was very intelligent and bright, though perhaps bright is not the right word, because he was also very dull, in that he was an unhappy, repressed man. He had devoted his whole life to his patients because that was the one thing that made him feel worthwhile. He had been married for thirty years and had three children, but I got the impression that he never shared his feelings with his wife and used patients to barricade himself against her.

JOURNAL (December 1980) Ury gave me snippets he had written about himself—unbelievably moving. Some, inevitably, infantile memories, because that is where his whole orientation points him. But among them, some _new_ aspects—his numbness, the pain of coming back to feeling things again. This is what he wrote: "To become more aware is both to become more hopeful and also to experience pain—the experience which comes to mind is the pain in a limb when a tourniquet is removed; those parts which had ceased consciously to exist, suddenly scream out and flood one's awareness."

From the beginning of our relationship, my focus was on Ury. Every morning, when I woke up, I would lie in bed and plan what I was going to say to him. He was, to me, like one of my patients; I was convinced that my task was to help him move forward in his individuation. For Ury, this attention was welcome. He had not talked about himself to anybody since his initial training as a psychoanalyst twenty-five years ago. He shared with me accounts of his childhood, his relationship with his brothers, the disturbing experience of leaving Germany and coming to England at the age of 9 and the even more disturbing experience of being interned with his family on the Isle of Man. When the war was over, he trained as a doctor, and subsequently had analysis and training at the Institute of Psychoanalysis. His life had been exclusively work. This is what he loved, and this is what he wanted to talk about. He didn't have any interests outside psychiatry.

To me, it was all fascinating and I felt very privileged to be hearing about it. Although the focus of our relationship was on his development, in fact it had a transforming effect upon me. As the weeks progressed, we became deeply involved with each other. Not sexually. I don't remember at that time any physical contact between us, but psychologically we became very close. For the first time in my life, I felt I was loved. It felt exhilarating and liberating. I would lie in bed and feel my body tingling with life. I started to think about my appearance because I wanted to appear attractive to Ury. Instead of the jeans, T-shirts, and jumpers I had worn for years, I started to go to charity shops and buy designer clothes. I bought rings and earrings from the market. I had never bothered about my appearance before, in fact didn't have any sense of style and was not interested in fashion. Now it became an important part of my life. I loved pondering what I was going to wear each morning. There were changes in Ury too. He had given up his pipe and he told me he was now having a bath every night instead once a week and he had started listening to music in the evenings.

We met as often as we could, sometimes in his office in the grounds of the hospital, sometimes at his home in Ealing in the evening—his family were used to him seeing patients then. Sometimes we went to a pub for lunch, sometimes for walks in the park or along the river. Always we were talking, talking, talking about ourselves. My focus was on him, but he was interested in me also. I found him very congenial and, from a psychological point of view, fascinating.

His pathology was typical of many intelligent men, the pathology of the *puer aeternus*. The *puer aeternus* is the eternal boy, the Peter Pan who never grows up and lives in the clouds, full of ideas and projects but never able to come down to earth and put them into practice. The *senex* is the opposite—the old man who is stuck in the mud, out of touch with vitality and creativity.

I learnt so much about male psychology through my relationship with Ury. I discovered that the *puer* needs supreme courage to come down to earth and live out his dreams in reality. Over the months and years of the relationship with Ury, I struggled to bring him down to earth.

JOURNAL (January 1981) More centred now—though sometimes when I think of Ury and me, it seems very unreal. Last night, at the Tanner's dinner party, I felt as if I was living in two worlds concurrently. Could it really be so, what I was experiencing with Ury? I am beginning to realise that it is to do with growing and stretching my emotional capacity; there is room in my life for Francis and Ury. I am not taking anything away from Francis, and, in a way, will have more to give him. But, at the moment, I still feel very unsure. The emotional turmoil this is causing me makes university work exceedingly difficult and exams are in a fortnight's time. I am complacent enough to feel I will not fail, but sometimes I feel sad at my lack of motivation and concentration because I could have done well. But if I were given the opportunities I have had since September all over again (i.e. Sasha, Ury, patients) I would do the same again! Where is it taking me? To being a more whole person. It is a quest for totality—for Ury and for me. He is finding parts of himself he had lost and so am I—and this is what we are giving each other.

I think, at that time, I was extraordinarily boring and one track minded in my thinking. Ury's individuation was my overwhelming concern. All our conversations centred around this, me probing and prodding him, persuading him to move forward. He never seemed exasperated by me, never said, "For goodness sake, let's talk about something more interesting like the theatre, music or books." The only books we discussed were about psychology, and unless we were talking about patients, our conversation was about ourselves, particularly him. This was not because he was self-centred. He knew I was seeing Sasha twice a week and could share my own problems with him. Ury had not talked about himself for years. He loved his wife and his brothers and his children. But this was not the sort of conversation he could have with them. Ury thought I was wonderful. I was bringing him to life, opening doors, and showing him the possibility of finding new ways of living.

JOURNAL (March 1981) "I feel like a swim," Ury said, stretching his arms out—and then we spent the afternoon exploring together, swimming in the unconscious, it seemed to me. Yes, we are moving—he is starting to feel—in his way and at his pace. When I start to push, it is totally misplaced and counterproductive. His growth—and mine as part of it—gives me exceptional feelings of happiness and exhilaration. It is like being in love, but it is not that. It is the joy of being centred, and loving, and being acknowledged—moving one tiny section of humanity (Ury and me) one step nearer God.

To begin with, Ury used psychoanalytic interpretations about himself because that was his orientation and training. My interpretations were strange to him, but after a time he welcomed them as a breath of fresh air. Increasingly he became interested in Jungian psychology, so much so that he bought the twelve volumes of Jung's collected works. I tried not to burden him with Jungian theory, but this is what I was fascinated by and inevitably our conversation returned to it time and time again. I had this fantasy that Ury would heal the *puer-senex* split in himself, come down to earth and join the Jungian group in London, to which he would bring a wealth of experience.

JOURNAL (April 1981) Ury is on holiday. I think a lot about him and wonder where he has got to and where our relationship will take us. I ask myself why I continually remind myself about his negative qualities and rarely acknowledge the positive. Why? Is it because the negative is more apparent? I think not—this is something to do with me. Is this a defence? Am I scared of going head over heels with him? Maybe, that's it. As I write this, I can sense a part of me saying, with a sneer, "Head over heels for that little man!" So Ury is carrying negative projections too. Because, if he is to change and grow, I must see and acknowledge the positive in him. Why do I automatically assume any ideas he has won't be any good? Why do I not expect him to be a 'good' lover? Why do I not expect adequate masculine behaviour from him? Because he has not yet been able to do any of these? That is true so far—but never? I think my reaction to Ury is connected to how I felt about Geoffrey—I came to see what an inadequate man he was and loved him in spite of it. I never expected him to be different. But this is not the case with Ury; he can be different. The more I expect from him, the more he will give. I need to concentrate on the positive, not on the negative.

When I finished at Brunel, having graduated with an upper second class honours degree, Ury offered me a job as a psychotherapist at Ashford Hospital, in a new psychiatric unit on the outskirts of London where he was a consultant. Also, at this time, I went to a four-day conference in Oxford: four days talking about dreams with Jungian analysts, led by Jung's pupil, Marie-Louise von Franz. It was a stimulating, engrossing and confidence-giving experience. I felt accepted as a colleague, and I was able to see that fundamentally what is important in our work is who we are, our personality, the totality of our experience.

JOURNAL (September 1981) I started the job at Ashford hospital yesterday—amazingly fortunate to have an NHS appointment as a psychotherapist. Many people in Oxford expressed envy. It will be a challenge and very difficult at the beginning as it is a new unit, and everybody is very unsure of themselves.

The relationship with Ury was not only transforming and exhilarating, over time it also became incredibly frustrating as I urged him forward and he stuck terrified in his tracks. He loved the idea of progress, of living in a new way, and of being more adventurous, but he seemed unable to put his ideas into practice. Sometimes I felt hopeful that he would loosen the stranglehold of the *puer aeternus*. But he seemed unable to do this. I thought the only way forward—the only way to free him from the stranglehold that was holding him back—was for our relationship to become sexual. At first, I was very unsure about this and had made many agonised entries in my journal about it. I knew Ury was stuck. I knew that there was a barrier stopping us exploring further. I also felt great pressure on me to move the relationship forward and felt this could only be done if we became lovers. This, I was convinced, would bring Ury down to earth.

JOURNAL (October 1981) I don't want to have an affair with Ury. I don't find him physically attractive, and I value my marriage above anything else and believe an affair would harm it. So why am I even contemplating it? It seems like a car I've started, and I can't stop and get out. I've got this relationship with Ury going (and it was right that I did so, I can see that for both of us) but now it has gained momentum and that is what is frightening me. I'm finding a depth of exploration and sharing with Ury I cannot find with Francis. I have handed my sexuality over to Francis and it has been fine for me that way. Maybe, to become a whole woman, I've got to take it back.

Ury and I both wanted to become lovers, at least he said he wanted to. But the logistics of our lives made it difficult to achieve. There was one fateful weekend when I was alone at home because

Francis had taken the children to see his parents. Ury's wife had gone to Germany with her choir. It was a wonderful opportunity to move our relationship forward.

When the weekend arrived, Ury came to my house for supper. He seemed very tense and jumpy and after a couple of hours, said he didn't feel well and had to go home. I felt numb with misery. Here was this perfect opportunity, we wouldn't get another chance like this, and he was running away. But I said nothing and commiserated with him for not feeling well.

Over the next few days, I was supportive and kind to Ury, who told me how much he had learnt from the weekend, talked about it being hard work, and that he was seeing things about himself in a new way. He said that the night he had left me, he had a dream that he was on top of a hundred storey skyscraper, and I was standing below, saying to him "jump". He said the most terrifying moment had been when I had asked him why he was there and he found himself on the point of replying, "Because you asked me." He said he realised then how passive he was, how unconfident and unable to initiate. He thought this was because he had been rejected so often.

My feelings of misery and anger at Ury's cowardice were bottled up inside me. I was kind and sympathetic to him but felt numb for several days. My feelings about the weekend burst out into my journal a few days later.

JOURNAL (April 1981) I am angry, angry, angry. Why should I waste my time with this timid fraud of a man? How long do I go along with it? If I hold a gun to his head, he will respond, but that's how it always is with him—he only responds and does not initiate. There is no way out of this impasse for him and me—so I go on alone. But where to and to whom? Because, I realise, I cannot do this exploration on my own. Passionate transformation, that's what it is about— and passion is a reciprocal thing—it needs two. I'm feeling now so frustrated at his inability to explore with me. Putting his toes in—just enough to keep me happy—but no more. It leaves me with a feeling of fury. Oh God, how do I channel this? Use it? Do with it? I want to grow and thrive and reach up into the sky exultantly and blossom and I cannot do it on my own. I'm tethered to this frightened and cowardly man, who hasn't even got the guts to say he loves me.

The following evening, I started to do an active imagination and a dragon emerged. (In the next chapter, I explain how I learnt to use active imaginations to explore the unconscious.)

ACTIVE IMAGINATION Huge, fierce, fire snorting from nostrils. I can hardly believe my eyes. I don't feel frightened, just amazed that such a thing really exists and in such an inconspicuous place—on a beach of a seaside town. The dragon curls up on the beach, its tail twisted around it, spiked, green, quite large. I take a long stick and poke it. It opens one eye and looks at me. I am determined to provoke it. I want to take it on. So, I poke it again quite hard. It snarls threateningly.

"Come on!" I say. "I'm not scared of you. Do your damnedest." I stand in front of it and can feel the fire from its nostrils and see inside its cavernous mouth. It snaps and snarls at me.

"Go on. Eat me!" I say. "I'm not scared of you." And, extraordinarily enough, I'm not. I stand there with my arms folded across my chest, waiting for the dragon to do whatever he wants. But he does nothing. He seems bored by my defiance. So, he settles down to sleep and I sit on his head in a nonchalant manner to display to the world that I am not frightened of the dragon and can do anything I want with him.

The dragon represents the fury inside me from Ury's rejection; and beyond that, the bottled-up anger and pain that had been inside me for years. By getting in touch with the dragon, through active imagination, I was able to bring the feelings into consciousness.

I felt an enormous sense of relief at facing my rage and possible destructiveness. Sitting on the dragon's head showed I was now in touch with my dragon and able to control it.

This gave me the strength and confidence to leave the anger from the abortive weekend behind and to urge Ury to move forward because I knew there was more for us to explore. The relationship had been transformative and exhilarating for me but now it was becoming frustrating as Ury stuck rigid with fear at the prospect at any change. But I didn't give up; I continued to urge him forward, and when we eventually did become lovers, I was amazed at the change in Ury. It seemed to free him, to release something in him that had been blocked. For the first time since we had been together, he started to dream prolifically. Each time we met, he brought his dream notebook with him, and we worked on his dreams together. At last, I thought, *at last*, Ury has started on the path of individuation. It was as if by being courageous and taking this huge step, he had freed himself and had released a barrier within. He was starting to combine the *puer* with the *senex*, the eternal boy with the old man. At last, Ury was coming down to earth.

I felt I was using all my skills with Ury. He kept me on my toes—I never knew how he would be from one day to the next; sometimes he was full of enthusiasm and ideas, and then the next day would be sunk in gloom about life and himself. He seemed incapable of stepping outside his rut. When he tentatively ventured out, I wondered how much of his movement was just to please me.

JOURNAL (June 1981) I feel overwhelmed and exhilarated by what is happening to Ury. I never dared to hope this would really happen and yet it was at the bottom of my heart from the beginning and foreshadowed in that dream when he borrowed the ladder. He is actually working at his individuation—by recording his dreams and drawings and now he is reading Jung. First, Marie-Louise von Franz on Alchemy—and now Jung. He is amazingly open and receptive to

Jungian ideas. Of course, Ury and I are on the same wavelength—we share so much in common from a psychological point of view that is not very surprising that he should be attracted to Jung. But I have to distinguish between the fantasy and the reality; the fantasy is the Ury with whom I share my ideas, whom I love, who shares my development. The reality is a shrivelled up, sad, cowardly psychiatrist. But what is happening? Fantasy and reality, in a miraculous way, are coming together. It gives me great joy to see him growing and coming to life and starting to find himself once more.

From the beginning, the relationship with Ury was full of contradictions: on the positive side, he was my boss, a psychiatrist and psychoanalyst, I felt proud to be in a relationship with him and it gave me a feeling of status and of security. On the negative side, when I saw him with other people, he seemed unimpressive, unattractive, and I wondered why on earth I was in a relationship with him. I was also very critical of him: I told myself he was cowardly and unadventurous, stuck in the mud, full of ideas but not able to put them into practice. But when Ury and I were alone together, I felt very differently. He was my soulmate; I could say anything to him; he was very easy to talk to, very receptive and understanding, and his admiration of me made me feel feminine and appreciated. When we were making love, I found him attractive; he was everything I wanted.

The relationship continued over the next three years in fits and starts. Sometimes I felt very optimistic about Ury and thought he was changing and moving forward. At other times I was frustrated and fed up with him because of his small-mindedness. The urgency that had pushed me towards Ury was no longer there. Although this secret relationship in the centre of my life gave me a feeling of worth and purpose, I also felt restricted and tethered by Ury. He wanted me as his girlfriend, nothing was going to rock the boat of his marriage. I had no wish for this either, but wasn't content to jog along in a comfortable relationship. For me, the relationship was all about growth—his and mine. I expressed my frustration in my journal.

JOURNAL (September 1982) Why do I bother with a man who tells me he is thinking about me but cannot make a 20-minute journey to see me? Why go on caring passionately, loving, yearning, striving, hoping? Because in doing so, I am pushing myself to my utmost limits. Through the pain, I am learning about myself. But bugger him! Why can't he make it a bit easier? Do one thing I don't expect.

So what is happening here? My gloves are off—no more pretence—I am going to try to be straight with him. When he makes me unhappy, when I need him, I will say so. It means no longer being the good mother and pandering to the little boy. Instead, I am being a woman, a passionate, emotional woman with needs. This is what he has never known (at least with me and I suspect with others) and it is a role I don't know myself very well. It requires considerable honesty and consciousness because the dangers are manipulation, power, seduction for my own needs. But Ury has to be seduced, cajoled, and forced to grow up, and that is why my gloves have come off and I shall no longer be the nourishing mother.

When I realised that for Ury our relationship was a pleasant and enjoyable side issue of his life, and that for all his promises and good intentions, he had no inclination to change anything, I started to withdraw from him. On his part, when he realised what was happening, he started to punish me in his typically small-minded way, by "forgetting" that we were having lunch on a certain day, or by referring an impossible and unhelpable patient to me. He didn't dare confront me. And as I became more aware of this, I realised with great sadness, I had to move forward on my own.

JOURNAL (May 1983) I am offering him all of myself and he's only picking out the easy, acceptable bits. He is a coward, will do nothing new that may rock the boat—so the frills, the fun, the periphery are OK for him—but nothing requiring change—and therefore no real transformation. And that is what I offer. The other any attractive, seductive woman could have given him. But I am more than that. I am willing to walk into the fire with him—to go all the way—to venture into unknown territory—and few people would do that. But because he is a coward, he cannot accept what I have to offer—and that makes me feel very lonely and undervalued and under-stretched and frustrated.

For every seed that germinates, there are dozens that fall on hard ground and die. Is that my fate? The ground is very hard. He does not see what I have to offer. I am beginning to wonder if it is there at all. What is it that is pounding at my heart? I cannot take this sterile, unadventurous, confined relationship. I can't <u>stand</u> to be restricted like this. He is a coward—a bloody feeble coward. No Hercules he. He's never going to move out of his prison—he will open the windows and start seeing the view, but no more than this will he do.

The prospect of ending the relationship with Ury scared me; mostly I was scared of the loneliness. He was such a comforting presence, so reassuring. He made me feel good—a confidante I could share my worries and thoughts with—but I knew I had to move on. If I stayed, he would encase me in concrete.

One Friday evening at his house, he was telling me about one of his patients that he'd seen that morning. I was tired and didn't want to hear about this. I wanted him to talk about himself, to be telling me about his dreams, to show me he was moving forward. The room seemed characterless and without colour. I had been there many times before but had never registered that the walls were beige coloured and so was the furniture. Suddenly, out of my mouth, burst all the things I had been saying to myself over the past months.

"You're a coward. You're running away from your potential. Nothing has changed. You're still stuck in a rut. You are not making any effort to move. There is no point in continuing this relationship."

Ury looked shaken and frightened. Immediately, I wished I hadn't lost my temper. I apologised.

"I'm tired, let's forget it." And I left soon afterwards.

Over the weekend, I felt miserable about what I had done. I thought that I had killed the relationship. But, on Monday, when we met for lunch, to my amazement, Ury told me he had a vision on Saturday morning which had changed his perception and he now saw what a clot he had been—and he apologised to me. He gave me some beautiful flowers—enchantment lilies—and said he felt terribly sad and tired. At first, my reaction was that it was not real, but, as he talked, I could see it was. It seemed like a miracle.

Ury's vision was of a Madonna (like Leonardo or Michelangelo, he said) holding a child, royally dressed in beautiful clothes—holding it out to him. Then he saw that he had stripped the child of all its clothes and reduced it to a mere child. This showed him, he said, what he had been doing—and he understood why. He was frightened of being taken in by people. When he was young, he had projected the magical into his parents, and when he discovered they were fallible, ordinary people, he felt let down and adrift. He lost his confidence in life because he could no longer trust his parents. When the whole family were banished to the Isle of Man during the war, this accentuated the problem. Then he lost confidence in his new country as well. The vision showed him that because of this he had stripped his life of all colour and meaning. This was why he was so reluctant to take initiatives. This was why he tried to control everything himself. He now saw that the whole stalemate in his life was a spiritual problem.

I felt overwhelmed with joy about what Ury told me. It was a miracle and I thought it was going to transform his life.

Shortly after this extraordinary breakthrough, Ury went on holiday to Norway with his wife. Usually when he was away, he would write to me every other day. After nine days, when I had received no letters, I began to worry that he was ill or even may have died. I realised I would be the last person to know if this was the case. I worried that the breakthrough had killed him. If he really acknowledged what he saw, the implications were considerable. There was a mountain for him to climb but I was sure that he could do it if he was committed and held onto that wonderful vision.

Ury didn't die on holiday. The night after he got back, I went to see him at his home. I took with me, as a present, a small picture of the Madonna of Peace which I had bought at the Medici Gallery many years before. When, before his holiday, he told me about his vision, this beautiful picture had come into my mind, and I wanted him to have it.

He was pleased to see me and had brought back a little present. I was holding my breath with anticipation, waiting to hear where he had got to, not on his travels with his wife, but on his inner journey. But, as he talked about his holiday, I began to see that Ury had switched off and become small-minded again. With a sinking heart, I saw that Ury had brushed the vision aside. I realised then that there was no future for us and that I had to go on alone. I gave him my picture of the Madonna of Peace and immediately wished that I hadn't. He, characteristically, hid it under the wrapping paper so that his wife wouldn't see it. That for me was the last straw. He was unable to acknowledge his vision and he didn't want his wife to know about it. Not writing to me for two weeks was an indication, as was the present he brought back for me—a very unspecial trinket and the way he talked about his holiday: completely switched off on his own development. His emotion and apology and the flowers from two weeks ago seemed like another world.

JOURNAL (July 1983) How could it happen? How could God let it happen, after breaking through to him like that? I think it is narcissism that grips him and puts a block on God. There is no way God can enter him if Ury takes upon himself God-like qualities. Now, what for me? On—on my own—I've got to find my own inner man. Tears, tremendous pain tonight. I know I have to let Ury go and move on. I feel great pain. I feel I have given everything to bring him to life: my love, myself, everything, and I have failed.

I feel so sad at the blindness of human beings and their inability to step out of their prison. But that sadness puzzles me. Why should I weep about this when far more appalling tragedies occur in the world every day? I feel I must be weeping on my own account. Because of human frailty, I have to go on alone. There never will be a companion to share my journey with. I am infinitely blessed in my marriage and children. This is far more than most people have. My spiritual journey has to be alone.

EXPLORING THE UNCONSCIOUS

I DO NOT understand the connection between starting the relationship with Ury and being able to explore the unconscious but that is what happened. Maybe, by taking one decisive step, I was then ready for the next. At that time, my dreams started to challenge me to explore further:

DREAM I decide to take the children out for a walk. In the car I forget to turn left in time so instead take a turning down road that leads to a cul-de-sac by a new sports centre. We get out and I lead the children through to the sports ground. It is dark. A man's voice shouts, "What the hell are you doing? Get out!" He comes rushing over—a dark, thin, young man, beaky face—talks very rudely to me. I am not prepared to listen to that sort of talk and walk away. I go towards sports centre where he came from. A man is bending over engine (bonnet open) of his car. I introduce myself and he immediately knows who I am. I also know who he is. He is attractive, fairish, but strange, oddly slanting eyes.

This dream shows both negative and positive aspects of the animus as I venture into the unconscious. It also shows that I am able to stand up to negativity. Hermes, the man with the strange oddly slanting eyes, becomes an important guide. I can't remember how the man in the dream became Hermes, but I knew that was his name, and his image and personality were firmly fixed in my mind.

A few days later, sitting in one of the armchairs in my study, after the little children had gone to bed and the older ones were watching TV, I started writing in a notebook the thoughts that were coming into my head. I wrote a quotation from Auden at the top of the page. The sports centre was still vivid in my mind. With a large A4 notebook on my lap, I shut my eyes and it was as if I was on the sports field. I tried to write down what I was experiencing, without thinking critically about it. This is what I wrote that evening:

"How do I know what I think until I see what I say?" (Auden)

I go to sports centre again and walk through alleyway and go to find Hermes—he tells me to explore—he puts on light for me so I can see the whole of the playing field and he says he'll come to join me in a minute. It is a huge square place—green grass—trees round edge, a bit like a cricket field—and at edge there is a lake—with gondola-like boats on it—nobody on them—and a bridge across to an island. I go across to it. On island, there are four trees with birds' nests in them— and a hammock slung between two of them. Hermes comes across and tells me to get into hammock—it is lovely and warm and I lie in the sun basking and I ask him about himself—and what he wants of me—and he says he has a lot to teach me, many, many things to show me but we are in no hurry—there's lots of time, the world is at our feet and we will explore it together. I say to him that I don't know if I'm listening to him in the right way and he says to take it easy, to bask in the sun and things will take their course. "I'm impatient," I say. "I want to go down deep and explore." He says, "You can't force the pace. There is a right time and a right way of doing things."

Looking back on what I had written, I realised it was what Jung calls active imagination. In *Memories* he describes how active imagination is a useful technique for approaching the unconscious, but he doesn't advise how to go about it. I was excited by my first attempt. After that, I tried to do active imaginations whenever I had time on my own. I experimented and devised my own method and over time became more confident in using it. I had a special notebook for this and wrote with a purple felt-tipped pen. Sinking down into myself, I wrote down the images that came into my mind. A lot of what I wrote is nearly illegible because I was writing with my eyes shut. All the time I was doing this, doubt dogged me. Was I making this all up? I wondered. Was this just my imagination? Or was I, in fact, making contact with the unconscious?

In spite of my doubts, I continued to write active imaginations in the evenings. They became an absorbing part of my life. I didn't talk about them with Ury because I didn't think he would understand. Sometimes I would read an active imagination to Sasha, and he would jot down notes as I did so. Once, when we were discussing one, he said what I was doing was unusual. As far as I was concerned, everybody in a Jungian analysis was doing active imaginations, but apparently this was not the case.

I soon discovered that active imaginations, like dreams, were unpredictable and did not come when I wanted them to. Sometimes I would sit, pen in hand, ready to write, but there was nothing there; my mind seemed completely blank, I could not write down anything. At other times, I wrote copiously, but when I looked back a week or so later at what I had written, I realised they were not active imaginations, they were written by the ego—they were contrived. The difference was easy to spot—not at the time of writing them, but afterwards looking back. The contrived active imaginations read like stories I was telling myself; the material came from things I knew. The genuine active imaginations had a feeling of vibrancy with figures and places I did not know. They were surprising and often disturbing. The guides in the genuine active imaginations, Hermes and his assistants, frog, dwarf and goldfish, were powerful figures for me and when they appeared, I felt a frisson of excitement. Most evenings, I would try to enter this strange world. Sometimes I would find myself going through a trap door, down into the bowels of the earth; at other times I was exploring a beautiful garden. I saw many strange things—such as a huge snake, curling round and round on the bottom of the sea. Sometimes I was lying in a hammock on an island, just basking in the sun. Hermes was my main guide, but there were also others. Frog took me on many extraordinary adventures. He was very large, nearly as big as me. At first, I was repulsed by him. His hands were slimy and made me shudder. But, as I got to know him, he became a trusted guide.

Doubt about what I was doing was always at the back of my mind. Was I making it all up, imagining these extraordinary figures? I asked Hermes about this:

ACTIVE IMAGINATION "I don't ask to understand the meaning of everything. What frightens me is my own self-deception—can I hoodwink myself? I can put up with greyness, unhappiness, difficulties—but what defeats me is myself. Am I playing games with myself? Is this just a sort of self-deception?"

There was a large hole in the ground in front of me, full of warm water, bubbling—a bit like washing up water, mud coloured. I put both my hands in it—it was reassuringly warm. There were several stones and pebbles in the water and Hermes was standing beside me. He said, "We are washing you in the water like the pebbles. Putting your hands in the water is like Thomas putting his hands in Christ's side. Does it help you to accept the reality of the psyche?"

During the day, my life carried on as usual—cooking, shopping, taking the cat to the vet, fetching children from school, seeing a few patients at the outpatient clinic in the hospital, having lunch with Ury. But all the time the active imaginations were in my mind, an extraordinary world that I was exploring. I longed for the evenings. Active imaginations became far more important to me than anything else in my life.

Some active imaginations, like dreams, spoke directly to me and addressed problems in my life. In one active imagination I found myself walking down a road. I didn't want to, and it was quite an effort, dragging my feet along, struggling to lift them, my shoes felt too large and heavy. I asked Hermes what I was doing wrong. He told me I was trying too hard.

Another time, I was shown the danger of being in touch with the unconscious. I saw a hammock swinging from the moon in the sky. I jumped up into the sky and sat with the moon in the hammock. I felt quite giddy up there and saw drops of blood fall from the hammock onto the earth below. When I tried to leave the moon, to return to the earth, my foot became entangled in the netting of the hammock, and I panicked as I tried to free myself. When I got back to the earth, I saw a rope ladder hanging down from the hammock, inviting me to climb up to the moon again. The feeling of being entangled in the netting was very frightening, and my panic as I tried to disentangle my foot stayed with me. It was a warning of the danger of inflation, of getting too close to archetypes. I realised I must not be seduced by the rope ladder hanging down from the moon. I needed to keep my feet firmly on the ground.

My lack of confidence was a continual theme. When I complained to the dwarf, he said to me, "Stuff and nonsense" and prodded me with his stick. "Who wants to be confident? It is only skin deep."

ACTIVE IMAGINATION The dwarf shows me a bridge on which is a beautiful thing like a huge vessel—the sort of thing you see in an Eastern temple—interwoven strands of gold, very fine craftsmanship—a sort of gold latticework—and then a scroll or knobs on top—and two gold rings/handles on either side. It is standing on the edge of the bridge—shining with a lovely glow and incense is coming out of it—the smell is not incense but a heavenly smell—more like a perfume of flowers. "Go on. Have a good look," said the little man, poking me with his stick. I walk up onto the bridge and look at the beautiful object—it is taller than me—I gaze up at it, inhaling the lovely smell. There are waves in the lake beneath the bridge which make a lapping sound against the shore—and then I see that a whole host of white birds are sitting along the shore—crowds of them.

This active imagination encapsulates the essence of individuation. I am shown the beautiful vessel on the bridge with white birds on the shore—both symbols of the Self, the unique centre of the personality. My lack of confidence and inability to see where I was going were ego problems.

One evening, the dwarf led me to a bleak courtyard, where I was put in touch with rejected parts of my personality.

ACTIVE IMAGINATION All around are cell doors—people's faces, pressed against the grills, looking at me. There does not seem to be any way out of the courtyard. Every part is taken up by cells and grills. I walk round to see if one is empty so I can get through. But in each one there is a prisoner, unshaven, sinister, mute, staring at me. I look for my little guide but he has gone. I am very angry. I shout, "Where are you? Come back! Don't leave me here." My voice echoes round and round the courtyard. So what am I to do? The only way out seems to be through one of the cells. To do this, I would have to make contact with the convicts. But I am frightened; the men look very dangerous and wild. I grit my teeth and go to open one of the doors. The man inside looks pathetic, his cell stinks, he is shaky, white-faced, scared of me, blinking at the unaccustomed sunlight. "It's alright. You can come out," I say, and he stumbles out into the sunlight and sits on the cobbled stones.

Why had I been frightened of him? And so it is with the others. Behind their grills, they look frightening but not when they come out; just dirty, dishevelled, unconfident men. Then I realise that I could easily get out because I have the keys to the cell doors.

When I re-read active imaginations, they often bring tears to my eyes, but I realise this is because they are my experience of the unconscious. For many people, the symbolism is strange and bewildering. Although we are all grounded in the collective unconscious, each of us will have our own individual experiences; I cannot expect mine to resonate with other people as they do with me. Therefore, in this book, although I have quoted from a few, I have included only two active imaginations in their entirety. These are the ones that changed the course of my life.

The following active imagination is one of them. It disturbed me greatly. It started in an amusing way, like a children's story, but then turned into something quite different.

ACTIVE IMAGINATION Four animals, different shapes and sizes, sitting near a pond, facing each other—comic-looking, like in a children's book. Passing round a pipe—having a yaw-yaw—about some serious topic. I go and sit beside the animals, listening to their talk, because I sense what they are saying is important for me to know.

The giraffe says, "It is intolerable, all this waiting."

"I don't think it is so bad," says mouse.

"It's because we are animals," giraffe says. "Nobody takes us seriously."

"I doubt if that is the reason," says the hippo. "It seems more how you view your time. Personally, I don't feel I have been kept waiting. Life stretches both forwards and backwards—what is the hurry?"

"It's the lack of consideration I object to," giraffe mutters.

"What is the problem?" I ask badger (who hasn't yet spoken).

"Well, it's like this," he says, in a deep, gruff voice. "We have been waiting a long time—some of us object more than others—others are more philosophic, you might say."

"What are you waiting for?" I ask.

"To be put in a box, nice and secure and made use of—we're wasted as we are—we need to be contained—not diluted."

"I'll find you a box," I say. I go to the dustbin and bring back a large box and they all get in and I do it up into a neat package and I leave it at the side of a mole hill.

"Are you OK?" I shout through to them, and I can hear four voices saying, "Yes."

After a day or two, the box starts to vibrate and move. I think the animals want to get out—so I go over.

"Keep away! Leave us alone!" one of them shouts. I keep away and watch. The box shudders and shakes and heaves and groans and then subsides into a black pool of oil—nothing there at all—and then above—a vision—a beautiful image floating in the sky of heavenly things. I fall down on my knees and worship it because it is a heavenly vision.

I hear a voice say, "Oh daughter of Zion, why are you so faithless! You know your task, follow your vision. What are you grovelling for? Stand upright—put your head high. Recognise yourself and recognise me, acknowledge me to the world. The walls of Judah will come tumbling down. The mighty will fall. Lion will lie down with birds and all creation will sing. How can you doubt when you know such things? How can you need any other acknowledgement? Let go of worldly values—hold fast onto inner strength—follow me—keep your eyes on me and let go of those props around you. Then your uncertainty, your worries, and anxieties will dispel. Hold fast to what you know to be true—let go of everything else. Pray and praise the Lord and be grateful for his creation. The birds, the garden, the children, are all fruits of his creation. You know this. Don't pretend it is otherwise. Keep your eyes on central values. Accept suffering and pray. That is the way of the cross."

What on earth was it about? I wondered. "Oh, daughter of Zion. Why are you so faithless?" The words went through me like a spear. Yes, it could be said I was a daughter of Zion. Yes, I had lost my faith. But here I was being challenged directly. "You know your task, follow your vision." It seemed unbearable to me; it was not how I saw myself and it was not how I wanted to be. When I read this active imagination to Sasha, I was shaking as I did so. Ever since that time in 1968 when I was ill and saw the visions on the cornice of the ceiling in my bedroom, I had turned against religion completely. I couldn't reconcile what I had experienced in the visions with the empty rituals of organised religion.

JOURNAL (January 1983) Belinda's confirmation on Saturday evening—a disappointing occasion.. Certainly, the numinous has left organised religion and one is left with an empty charade. Platitudes, mock-love for fellow man, Victorian rituals—bearing little resemblance to my experience of God. But as I sat there for three interminable hours, I realised that if organised religion did not exist, we would create it. We want/need to share our experiences.

Sasha helped me to see that the active imagination was forcing me to re-examine my attitude to spirituality. As a result, over the following months, many of the journal entries were pondering the relevance of Christianity and its connection to individuation. Was the Self the same as God? What was it that urged me forward along the path of individuation? Was this the same as the Holy Spirit? I needed to understand what I was experiencing and fit it in with what I knew and understood about psychology.

JOURNAL (January 1983) Is our relationship with the unconscious active or passive? Is it the ground of our being which we need to be in touch with? Is it instinctive and passive or is it more than this? Is there a loving God? Is this a myth—a story we tell ourselves? Does "he" take an active and personal interest in each one of us—or is what we experience an impersonal, instinctive ground, which gives us pleasurable sensations?

I did not share my explorations of spirituality with Ury. Partly because I felt on such shaky ground, but also because I didn't feel he would understand it.

JOURNAL (February 1983) Family life is very happy at the moment. There is a joyful feeling of harmony at home. All the children at home, all thriving in their own way. Simon, humorous, intelligent. Tina is learning how to hold her own. Alexander has gained a lot of confidence in the past month. Belinda has always had problems when Alexander is ill—it seems to hit a complex caused when he had meningitis; often, when he is ill, she is extremely difficult and throws scenes. But this week he has been ill, and Belinda has worked out, unconsciously I think, a way of coping with it. She has thrown herself into domesticity—helping me clean and cooking some quite difficult dishes all on her own.

In March 1983, there was a conference in Jerusalem of the International Association of Analytical Psychology. I was over the moon with delight when Ury said he would come with me to it. For him, conferences were an accepted part of his activities, his wife was used him going to them. For me, it seemed unbelievable that Ury and I would have ten days together. I booked a hotel room for us, which was separate from the English contingent.

But my sense of reality was skewed. To me, inner reality took precedence. I did not realise that outer appearances needed attention. All I could think about was Ury and me—ten days together—and also showing off to the AJA group this miraculous relationship. I did not think about how it would appear to them. The AJA trainees saw Virginia, supposedly happily married and with four children, parading her lover for all to see. Their shock and bewilderment caused serious repercussions. The AJA trainees at the conference would relay everything back to the Adlers, which would adversely affect my relationship with them and my training, as I describe in the next chapter.

⚜

Alchemists left notes for posterity
Crazy chemists
Notes make no sense
Scientifically.
They projected into the alembic
Their inner struggle
To find gold.
Not the hard, expensive yellow stuff
Weighed by jewellers
Sought by the avaricious,
The alchemists' gold
Was the Self
The gold in the centre of the personality
A natural process
Bringing together parts of the personality
Gold shines through and illuminates
But dangers lurk on the way
Abandoning old ways
Venturing into new territory
Dragons lie in wait for the unwary.

AJA

MY DECISION TO find another analyst and choose Sasha Duddington was in order to qualify for the AJA training. The Jungian training in London was fragmented. There were two main training schools and several subsidiaries. The difference between the two main schools, Association of Jungian Analysts (AJA) and Society of Analytic Psychology (SAP), was the degree of allegiance to the Zurich school where Jung had been based and where the original training scheme had begun. AJA, led by Gerhard Adler, one of the editors of the collected works of Jung, followed the model of the Zurich school. SAP, led by Michael Fordham, also one of the editors of the collected works, although based on Jungian ideas, was heavily influenced by Kleinian theory and embraced child psychotherapy.

My introduction to Jung had been through the Jung club in London, which was under the umbrella of the Jung club in Zurich; therefore I was attracted to the AJA training scheme, although the SAP was larger and more professionally run. In retrospect, I can see that life would have been much easier for me if I had joined the SAP training, chiefly because the analysts there did not know my mother. My mother was a very powerful personality, much loved by everyone who knew her. She was an extroverted feeling type, very good with people—unusual in the Jungian world which attracts introverts. But she was also prone to depression and had had years of analysis, first with Faye Pye and then with Gerhard Adler, both of whom became close friends.

After my experience with Faye, I should have seen the warning signals and avoided the AJA training, but I was irresistibly attracted to it—it felt to me to be my home, where I should be. This is why, after Faye died, I went to Sasha, who was vice-chairman of AJA. He was the only training analyst in the AJA camp who did not know my mother, and in this way, I felt I would be insulated from her influence.

The selection for the AJA training scheme took place in January 1983.

JOURNAL (January 1983) I have an interview with Gerhard Adler on Saturday for the AJA training. I am very pleased that he is interviewing me as I have always wanted to meet him and he has been a key person in many things that have affected me—as Mum's analyst, as the person Faye was fighting with, as the person who started the AJA training. If he takes against me, it will be tough for me—so I am nervous about meeting him. But I know that even if he won't have me in the training, it won't affect what I feel about myself or the direction I am heading. It will just make things harder. I wonder what he will question me about? How much Sasha has told him about me? My relationship with Faye, my relationship with my mother? I wonder, in fact, if he will be interested in me at all or if he will only talk about himself? Oh well, time will tell—but the young, unsure bit of me is anxious: What will he think of me?

Every time I met anybody who had connections with AJA and talked about how many applicants there were for the training, my heart would sink; I would go plummeting down, feeling insignificant, undervalued, and unwanted. I realised that my reaction was excessive: the fear of failing to get into the training scheme hit me deeply on an old wound and ignited the feelings inside me of the child who felt excluded and undervalued. AJA felt like my new family, and I dreaded being excluded from it. I reassured myself that Sasha valued me and made me feel worthwhile. If they didn't want me, I told myself, he would still stand by me. But I dreaded the thought of being excluded again. I longed to be accepted by the AJA family.

JOURNAL (January 1983) Shattering day yesterday. I have never felt like that before—really depressed—unable to think, in tears, the gloom overwhelming me, tremendous inner pain. I realise that the fear of being rejected by AJA brings back the childhood pain—all the feelings of not being acceptable.

"Why don't you want me? What have I done wrong? What have I got to do to join them? How can I get in? It seems that whatever I do, I'll never succeed—never get there—there will never be the acceptance and recognition I crave for. I know I can't be like Adam—I never will be a boy—but surely, I can be like Juliet? There must be a basic flaw in me. All the measuring up, the reassurances are to no avail. I will never be accepted."

This wound from childhood has made me assertive, anxious, insecure, competitive, obsessional, unsure. Last night as I sat alone in my study, I tried to go right into the pain and feel it all again (it was agony to do so). Then I realised that the way forward was to take that child in my arms and tell her that I love her. And that is what I did. I could feel her in my arms. I said to the suffering child within me, "You're lovely, I don't want you to be any different. I love you as you are. Let go of your anxiety and insecurity. Don't try so hard—there is no need. You don't need to be better than anybody else. You're you. You are fine as you are."

The miracle was that as I held her in my arms and spoke to her, my depression lifted, and the pain melted away. Now I feel at peace. I still mind very much about AJA, but not to the extent of feeling that life is not worth living if I do not get accepted.

When I was accepted by AJA, it felt like an anticlimax. So much libido had been invested in my struggle to accept possible rejection, that although I was very relieved, it did not feel important anymore. There was an initial meeting of the group in March. Then twice weekly seminars began in September.

In addition, as part of the training, we had to have weekly supervision of our casework by an analyst. I was allocated to Inge Allenby, an elderly analyst who lived in sheltered housing in Oxford.

I became disillusioned very quickly. AJA was not the happy family I had hoped for, it was not a mecca for Jung's ideas, and the trainees did not share their experience of the unconscious, as I had hoped they would. It was full of antagonism, tensions, conflicts, and rivalries. The quality of the teaching was poor—chiefly because there were not many analysts in the AJA group to call upon.

There was one exception, Barbara Somers, a charismatic woman, who was not a member of AJA. She worked independently and ran her own therapy organisation. She taught us for six seminars about archetypes, using mythology and fairy tales. I found her seminars absorbing and fascinating—so much so that in a moment of enthusiasm I told her about my active imaginations. She asked me to bring one to the next seminar.

Afterwards, I wondered whether I was right to mention them. Should I read an active imagination to the group? What will they think of me? Sasha was encouraging and so, at the next seminar, I read the active imagination about the box and the heavenly vision. I felt that Barbara had been on this path too. She made me feel accepted and that I had contributed usefully to the group. But this was not the case with the other trainees. They said nothing at the time or afterwards; I didn't know what they thought, but I felt unsupported by them. I wished I had not read the active imagination to them; in sharing my experience of the numinous, I felt exposed and very vulnerable. I wondered if they were laughing at me behind my back. What I longed for was sharing and recognition. "Yes, I've been there too. Yes, I know what you are describing." Barbara gave me this. I know she recognised the symbolism and had shared this journey, but not the others. They did not mention it at all, either then or afterwards. I felt they had brushed aside and discounted what I had shared.

My unhappiness in the group was not just on this occasion; there was something wrong with the group itself. It felt unsafe and unloving. When I had left AJA and could look back on those training seminars, I realised that the problem was caused by spies in the group: Hella Adler's analysands were telling her what was said. Her malign influence, running through the training scheme, which I experienced to my detriment, is now common knowledge. Also, there was something here to do with Jung which I found very distressing. This is where my heart was—his work was what I cared passionately about—and yet here, at the centre of his teaching, there was incompetence, malevolence, and decay.

At that time, I was trying to write about Jungian psychology—this stemmed from a desire to show colleagues in AJA that I was an admirable person—because delivering learned papers was the currency AJA valued. I was on the wrong path in trying to impress them. This was ego stuff. My journey was (and is) an inner one. This is what I had hoped to share with the group. Soon I became aware that none of them wanted to or were able to share my experience. I tried to meet them where they were, and in doing so blocked myself.

My work with patients continued to be an absorbing interest.

JOURNAL (July 1983) I am shocked by the way I behaved towards a patient on Monday. He is a man whom I have seen for four months, made considerable efforts on his behalf, and put myself out for him on various occasions. I rumbled the fact that it was all an act (at least, mostly) two weeks ago and confronted him with it. The subsequent session was better. But on Monday morning, I found myself freezing with antagonism. There was something in his manner, the way he manoeuvred and sidled around me—and as I saw this, I debated what to do: Point it out as I had done the previous week? Interpret? I did go through all the options, and then came to the conclusion it was pointless: he was using the sessions to allow himself to evade his responsibility. He wasn't being straight with me—in fact, he was deceiving me just as much as he deceived everybody else in his life. I thought, "No, this can't go on." I terminated the sessions.

I have felt bad about it ever since. Not that I was wrong—but I don't think it was right to end like that. I had said to him the sessions would end in August, but I sensed he was conning me—and if I said this to him, he would agree courteously and then continue to do so. On balance, I think I was right to do it, but not right in how I handled it. Should I have given him another appointment in a month's time? Reason and experience says, "yes". But something inside me shrieks, "no". And that's the bit that puzzles me.

Since that session, I have felt depressed about my work—I'm not sure if it is connected. The lovely feeling of confidence I've had for quite some time has gone—and I doubt my handling of Mr B. If I was wrong, I do not understand <u>why</u> I did it—because I am more than punctilious as a rule—a great stickler for doing things correctly. Was I reacting to a negative transference, as I did ineptly three years ago with that Sylvia person (and learnt a lot about transference, as a result)? No—it was as if something in me sensed that therapeutically I needed to chuck him out. He kept on licking my boots and asking me what he should say. Of course, it would make me feel a lot better if I knew it had put a bomb under him and was making him sort himself out. This afternoon, I even had a creepy doubt, when I came into the hospital, that he might have taken an overdose.

Soon after I joined the training scheme, I started to feel restless and dissatisfied in the analysis with Sasha. I knew something was wrong, I didn't look forward to the sessions as I used to, I often felt bored, as if something was missing. I told myself I needed to be confronted—on what I wasn't sure, but I knew Sasha couldn't do it. The problem was continually on my mind: what should I do about the analysis? Should I leave Sasha? But who else could I go to? Lots of my dreams addressed the problem.

DREAM I go to see Sasha and tell him I don't think situation is satisfactory. He agrees and takes a tough line with me. I can see he has probably been advised to make me conform. The problem is I can hardly understand him, his English is so poor and there is a noisy street outside with traffic.

DREAM I am in bed with Sasha and then he makes love to me. I'm not expecting it but gather he has intended to all along. It doesn't go very well—he says he can't get going properly. It leaves me with a nasty feeling. I don't feel Sasha is right to use the analytical relationship in this way.

I didn't realise it at the time but looking back now, I can see that the active imagination of the Cloak (see below), and Sasha's reaction to it, was the catalyst for my dissatisfaction with the analysis. This active imagination was a watershed moment for me. I felt overwhelmed and disorientated by it. At the time, I didn't understand its significance, but the images in it have never left me. I remember, as I read it to Sasha, I was shaking and tears were making it difficult to read. After the session, I felt embarrassed and uneasy about what had taken place, as if I had exposed myself in a most inappropriate way. It was this active imagination that led me to end the analysis with Sasha.

ACTIVE IMAGINATION Shell curling round and round encircling its pink nakedness. I climb inside the naked pink thing—round and round—in and in—deeper and deeper—softer and more vulnerable—no protection here at all—just soft and feminine and open and moist and loving and receiving—no barriers, no protection—but open—open to pain. Flowers can grow there—but oh so fragile—look where you step—take care—this is my centre—my heart—my love. Take care—treat it very gently—tread softly, respect it—it is a secret place—God is there—and he is small, still, very quiet, very silent and hidden. Brusque treatment will frighten him away and if you don't value this precious centre of me, I will feel a gaping wound is put through my heart. It has been shored up. Keep out. Danger notices have been there for years. There will be no explosions now. The bombs have been defused. But the pain is still there and I am very vulnerable. I am letting the hoardings go—and taking off the gloves—but the pink vulnerability—the awesome fragility is there. Please respect it. Don't harm this precious part of me.

I go further into the pink velvety texture—overpowering smell of narcissi. I walk gingerly in—very carefully, trying not to cause pain—it is very lush, very still and heavily perfumed in there. I part the veils with my hands and go in—parting the veils in front of me. I come to an opening—there are clouds all around—I put out my hand and touch one—a feeling of electricity tingles through me. Some babies lying on a rug in front of me—several of them—kicking—gurgling—happy. Some flowers and reeds nearby, bending over, heavy, water cascading gently onto rocks below. I take off all my clothes and roll in the water—there isn't very much—but somehow I want to cover myself in it—all over head, body, legs.

Then I go to lie beside the babies, lifting one up and placing it on my stomach—the pleasure of feeling its soft skin against mine. I feel long flowing hair against me—and looking up, I see, bending over me, a beautiful girl with long flaxen hair—drying me with her hair. I hand the baby to her and go over to put on my clothes— but instead of my ordinary clothes, find they have been replaced by flowing robes—red and black—rather like a wizard's outfit— hanging in folds from my shoulder. I rather fancy myself in it—and walk up and down, admiring my reflection in the water. Impressive I look. Some little maidens come running up and like bridesmaids hold up the end of my robe and we walk off in procession. People curtsey as I walk along, according me great respect. I am enjoying it but feel embarrassed and a fraud. I tell myself this is only me: they are curtseying to the Cloak; there is nothing fraudulent in wearing it—it was put out for me. If they want to curtsey, that's up to them. I'm still me—whatever I wear. That makes me feel better. But the uneasy feeling remains and I long to take off the Cloak and go back to being naked with the baby sitting on my stomach. That felt more real. But a voice seems to be telling me to keep up my procession and not to run away from the task of walking along, wearing the Cloak.

In the second paragraph of this active imagination, there is an overwhelming smell of narcissi. This would suggest that I am entering dangerous territory, the territory of narcissism. Here, Sasha was out of his depth and unable to help me. He had been a wonderfully sensitive and supportive analyst. He had helped me to start the relationship with Ury and had supported me as I ventured into the unconscious. But, in retrospect, I can see that it was his response to the active imagination of the Cloak that made me feel I had to get away from him, though none of this was conscious at the time. I told him that he wasn't strong enough for me, that I needed to be confronted. I realise now that it was not Sasha who needed to confront me but the reverse: I needed to confront him. At the time, I didn't understand the situation. Sasha was caught up in the archetype of the Cloak; for him I was more than Virginia. He had put me on a pedestal; he did not see the danger to me of identifying with the Cloak. Something in me recognised his blindness in this respect and that if I stayed with him, I would be trapped in his projection. What would have happened if I had confronted him? Could we have moved on together? Possibly. But it was not to be.

JOURNAL (May 1983) There is something worrying about what Sasha implied this morning—he was putting inner values on to outer events and they don't fit. Should they? The outer reality is that I am a middle-aged housewife, who has just completed a degree, who has had several years of experience in counselling and psychotherapy, and who is now at the beginning of training as an analyst. That is the outer reality. The inner reality is that I am getting in touch with parts of my psyche, parts which all women possess, which, he says, are rarely brought into consciousness. But inner wealth is not the same as outer wealth. It may well be that because of my inner journey, the outer will fall into place—but that does not necessarily follow. So Sasha jarred me by suggesting that I was not acknowledging the Priestess in me. This is not false modesty. It is reality. If he is saying that inner experiences are more important than outer qualifications, I agree with him. But the fact still remains, my inner experiences are hidden and private, known only to him and me. In the eyes of the world, I am what I appear to be.

Life would have been much easier for me if I had stayed with Sasha. He would have protected me from the Adlers' machinations. I would have completed the training course and would have become a qualified analyst. But that is not how things worked out. I've made many mistakes in my life, but leaving Sasha was not one of them; although it was against my own interests, it was an essential part of my individuation that made me move away from him. If I had stayed with Sasha, my life would have been relatively comfortable and easy, but I would not have developed as a person.

As usual, when faced with a problem, I consulted the *I Ching*.

Does the I Ching advise me to break away from Sasha?

Hexagram 28 (Preponderance of the Great)

"The load is too heavy for the strength of the supports. . .It is necessary to find a way of transition as quickly as possible and to take action. . .Nothing is to be achieved by forcible measures. The problem must be solved by gentle penetration to the meaning of the situation; the change over to other conditions will be successful."

Hexagram 29 (The Abysmal)

"Nothing can make it lose its own essential nature. It remains true to itself under all conditions. . .If one is sincere when confronted with difficulties, the heart can penetrate the meaning of the situation. But once we have gained inner mastery of a problem, it will come about naturally that the action we take will succeed. In danger all that counts is really carrying out all that has to be done–thoroughness–and going forward in order not to perish through tarrying in the danger."

I ended the analysis with Sasha in May 1983. After a lot of persuasion, and a wait of several months, I started analysis with Gerhard Adler in September 1983. I had read his books and admired his work as one of the editors of Jung's collected works. I had hoped that he would be everything that Sasha wasn't–intellectually stimulating and able to probe and push me further in my explorations.

Adler and his wife Hella lived in north London in a quiet road in a semi-detached house. This is where he saw his patients. When I arrived for my first session at the end of September, I waited outside the house until it was time for my session. I had been told to do this as there was no waiting room.

Gerhard Adler was a smallish man, bald, with a pronounced German accent. He was wearing large, obtrusive hearing aids and thick glasses. He sat in a reclining chair and, as we talked, he pushed the chair back so he was lying horizontally. Adler seemed very old and was keen to talk about my mother. She had analysed with him for several years, and afterwards had become a friend. In fact, she had been on holiday with Gerhard and Hella. To Gerhard, as to Faye, I was Nancy's daughter. Why on earth did I not see this? I had walked straight into a trap.

At that first session, Adler began to reminisce about my mother and her brother Jim. I sat patiently, in awe of this eminent man. After a couple of sessions, I started to tell him about my life.

"I'm happily married," I said, "and have four children."

"You're lying," he said, in his deep guttural German voice.

In the silence that followed, I could hear gurgles from his stomach, as he lay prone on his reclining chair. Had I misheard him? I was too much in awe of him, too bound up in wanting to be good girl to say, "What do you mean? Why do you say I am lying?" I retreated into myself, mumbled a few words, and left as soon as I could. I had told him virtually nothing about myself. I hadn't even begun to tell him about Ury, and he was calling me a liar. How could I work with someone who behaved like this?

Things quickly reached a crunch point with Adler over Ury. He and his wife would have learnt about my relationship with Ury from AJA members who were at the Jerusalem conference. It was because of this, Adler accused me of lying when I said I had a happy marriage. He did not realise that I was unconscious of the dysfunctional relationship with Francis. Although many of my dreams addressed the problem, I had not consciously accepted that the marriage was dysfunctional. I was hurt and dismayed when Adler said I was lying.

Over the next few weeks, I gritted my teeth and tried to get through to this man, to show him who I was. I brought him dreams and active imaginations, hoping they would show him the path I was travelling. He didn't seem to understand the dreams and about the active imaginations, he said to me, "Why are you bringing me these?" It became apparent that he had a fixed idea in his head about me. He said I had a power complex—inflated ideas of my own value—and needed "to be humbled." He implied that the seminar group did not like me.

JOURNAL (November 1983) I've got myself into this mess. At least *you* did—you've led me to this. Why? Out of the safety and warmth of Sasha—into this jungle where I feel scared, wondering who is going to jump at me next. I don't feel safe with him. He wants to hurt me, cause me pain, make me suffer. Why? In order to gratify his wife's need for power? "Make this girl have a negative transference. Show her who is boss. She is nothing—we'll show her." I won't let them destroy me. I value the precious part of me—and I will safeguard it. I will not let him near it. But how can I work with someone like this? Oh God, why have you landed me in this?

I regretted having said to Adler, at my initial interview, that Sasha was not strong enough for me. At the time, I felt uneasy about saying this because it felt disloyal to Sasha. Now, I realised, Adler was basing his attitude to me on this. He had to be strong—he had to make me weak. It seemed extraordinary that this eminent analyst had made assumptions about me without getting to know me and had acted on his assumptions in this very crude way.

The sessions became more and more fraught and frightening. I came to the conclusion that I couldn't work with him. I borrowed from my brother a hidden recorder that journalists use to record interviews. I took it with me to one of the sessions to record what Adler was saying to me, because I thought nobody would believe me. I never used those recordings, but they helped me to feel that if I had an opportunity to state my case, they would bear witness to what was happening. After six weeks, I terminated the analysis with Adler. I realised this would have repercussions on my training, but I thought I could find another analyst to take me on.

A week later, I received a letter from Adler apologising and asking me to return. But I had lost all confidence in him and felt threatened by him. I couldn't return to the analysis.

I was traumatised by my experience with Adler. What had I done to provoke such hostility—and not only from the Adlers? In the remaining months in the training group I felt antagonism and hostility. There was only one trainee who was sympathetic. She had also walked out from analysis with Gerhard Adler but had gone back after he had apologised. She never discussed it with me, but I thought she was congenial and wished I had known her better. All the others either ignored me or were rather caustic in response to anything I said. It was not a happy atmosphere.

After leaving Adler, I tried to find another analyst. Andrea Dykes agreed to take me on—but I sensed she also had been warned about me. I took this dream to her.

DREAM Our house is nearly finished. With Francis and children, we look at it—we've been decorating it ourselves. One room is not finished—the sitting room—it is rather dark and shabby. It is a huge room—taller than wide—the house is tower shaped and this room's ceiling goes to top of tower—and up the wall about 20–40 feet high, near top are some photos. I can see, with some imagination, we can make it very nice.

What is this dream about? I remember Andrea Dykes saying, "Oh, I don't like this," about the tower, implying that it showed inflation. Does it? When she said this, I remember feeling as if she was punching me below the belt. The fact I remember this forty years later, suggests to me that what she said was wrong. Another interpretation could be that parts of my personality are out of proportion. The tower represents the unconscious which is too large in relation to consciousness. The dream is saying I need to develop my conscious functioning.

I continued to go for supervision of my patients to Inge Allenby in Oxford. Here the antagonism and criticism were also apparent. I took her an interesting case of a university lecturer, who was working intently at his individuation. Allenby said he was grandiose and so was I, which rather took me aback—until I realised this came straight from Hella Adler.

This patient had been referred to me after he'd been admitted to hospital following an overdose. He was a very forceful, intelligent man, who had fallen in love with a secretary in his department. He had never spoken to her and didn't even know her name but was obsessed by her. His desperate longing to be with her, which consumed him day and night, and the hopelessness of this quest, led to him taking an overdose to end his life. It was obvious to me that his problem was the anima. He was out of touch with feelings and with the feminine part of his personality. Psyche was pushing him to recognise this, hence his obsession with the secretary. It was a fascinating case. Inge Allenby was wrong to say he was grandiose. She was misunderstanding his pathology. I found him a very rewarding but taxing patient, as shown by the following journal entry.

JOURNAL (February 1984) Having a set-to with AP in analysis—makes me really examine myself, my credentials, and what happened with Gerhard Adler. AP is in a full-blown negative transference. Very good for him and if I can sustain a steady course, will enable him to break through to feeling. He lammed into me this morning and made me feel very unconfident—he makes me feel unconfident anyway, because he is much cleverer than me, and because he is a powerful male. He tends to pull me into negative animus. He queried whether I knew what I was doing and my credentials for doing so—both sensitive areas with me. Qualifications are not my strong suit (and dammit, when he said how long have you been doing this, I answered him instead of interpreting—my only really bad mistake this morning.)

With AP, his psyche was ripe for this and was waiting for the opportunity which I gave him—by querying sexual fantasies. This released a stream of abuse at me. So I need to hold my own and interpret; know my Achilles heel is "bad girl" and also that I can handle AP as well as anybody could. I really *do* think so. I haven't years of experience behind me like Sasha or Hella, but I have human qualities that are unique to me: and I do know what I am doing. His is an archetypal projection i.e. the woman—seductress—betrayer—treacherer—can't be trusted—doesn't know what she's doing—will harm him. I have constellated his fear of the unconscious and the feminine—his whole anima problem. Absolutely essential that he goes through this and that I help him to see what it is about. I need to help him to express his criticisms and fear of *me* and then show him what they are really about. Woman—anima—was a repressed, wounded part of me for years. Now it is the most marvellous part—it has enabled me to bring Ury to life—and me too. Here with AP, I am really using the fruits of my individuation in analytic work.

Two months after I left the analysis with Gerhard, I received a letter from Hella Adler, as director of training, suspending me from the AJA program. The only course of action I could see was to ask Sasha's advice about what to do.

Sasha fitted me in at 8:30 a.m. before his other patients. Before I had a chance to explain to him what had happened, his phone rang and, uncharacteristically, he went to answer it in another room. In all the time I was seeing him, he never answered the phone during a session.

I couldn't hear what he was saying but, by the tone of his voice, I knew that he was speaking to Hella Adler. I should have left then. When he came back into the room, it was clear she had told him not to interfere. I realised there was no point in asking his advice.

I left Sasha's little consulting room, went home, and wrote a letter to Hella Adler, resigning from the training.

I felt devastated at leaving AJA, not only because I felt I had been treated very unfairly, but also because it was the end of my dream of being part of a Jungian organisation.

JOURNAL (February 1984) Terrible loneliness—and hurt about AJA and Sasha. I wish I could be like other people and belong to a group. This isolation and lack of support and people thinking badly of me is very hard to bear.

My future seems bleak because I so much wanted to contribute towards building a viable Jungian training—now that dream has come to an end. I feel very isolated and future-less and lacking in talent. I don't feel I have what it takes. I'm not particularly bright or imaginative or anything. Just an adequate analyst, who seems unable to get on with her contemporaries. Likening myself to predecessors, such as Jung or Neumann, is looking for support. If I feel I am in someone's footsteps, that feels better—then I feel success is assured. "They struggled, went through hell but then. . ." To struggle, alone and unwanted, with no hope of success, no aim in sight, is very difficult. No aim? Of course, there's always an aim—to understand, to redeem this, to come through it. Clinging to predecessors is like clinging to members of a group. "They are alright so I must be too." Being on my own feels bleak, defenceless, pointless. It is very difficult to stand firm and say, 'This is me, this is my raison d'être, these are my ideals.' It is much easier to belong to a group and have shared ideals so that when one falters, one is supported by the group.

I have invested AJA with something numinous. So have many others—there is unquestioning support by people like Sasha. He would not tolerate normally the things that are done under its aegis, but as it is AJA, he turns a blind eye. Why? Jung discusses this in The Practice of Psychotherapy. He says man is always searching for an outer vessel for inner divinity. This is what many of us have done with AJA—we have tried to create an outer vessel to contain the numinous.

Strange as it may seem, in the weeks following my departure from AJA, it was my relationship with Nancy and Juliet which occupied my thoughts. I felt that they would relish the fact that I had had to leave AJA. Why did it matter to me what they thought? In my journal, I tried to understand why I was frightened of their criticisms.

JOURNAL (May 1984) Why fear in relation to mother figures? My mother and sister will say, "There you are, Virginia has made a mess of things again." So have I got to prove to them I'm OK by *not* resigning from AJA? That's bloody silly. I was not doing the training to prove anything to Nancy, Juliet or anybody. But it seems I haven't faced the negative mother in myself. What is she like? Menacing, infiltrating, insidious, devious, manipulative, seductive, ensnaring, she will take me in and destroy me. This is the negative mother archetype.

What is the REALITY? Nancy and Juliet are both nice people who just happen to have a negative attitude to me. Most of the time they are in the background and 98% of the time I don't care what they think, at least this is the case when things are going well. When things go wrong, then I feel at their mercy. I feel they will be delighted and rub my nose in it. That's quite a neurotic bit of me—as if I need to be successful to *show* them—to keep negative mother at bay. I need to free myself from this. I need to detach archetype (negative mother) from carriers (Nancy and Juliet). Then I'll be able to be a success, flop, or whatever with equanimity.

Leaving AJA did not affect me professionally. I had a full private practice and an NHS job at Ashford Hospital. There I could choose the patients whom I thought I could help, and I was supported by a congenial team. Ury was reassuring about AJA. He said that it was an incompetent outfit, of little consequence, run by elderly people. In his opinion, I was well out of it.

At that time, I was trying to be more balanced in my relation to work. I wanted to get to the root of my compulsive caregiving—the need to be needed—not taking account of my needs and consequently neglecting myself and the family. It made me realise that this was the basic structure of my relationship with Ury. I had made superhuman efforts to meet his needs in order to be needed. Was I capable, I wondered, of a reciprocal relationship? It was me who had made all the efforts, all the sacrifices—to help him. This was not good for him—and it wasn't good for patients either. I was beginning to see that the abandoned child within me that longed to be loved and accepted was the cause of the compulsive caregiving. I didn't have the confidence to just be me—that did not seem enough. I had to learn, I told myself, that I didn't have to give all the time, for people to accept me.

JOURNAL (September 1984) The pain in my guts about not belonging is to do with the past not with the present. Compulsive giving, wanting to belong and be accepted, are neurotic parts of the old me. The way forward is up the mountain and I can only venture there if the old me—these neurotic needs and functioning—don't get in the way.

A year later, Jules, the only congenial member of the AJA training group, rang me to tell me that they had finished the training.

JOURNAL (March 1985) Talking to Jules on the phone this evening brings back the pain and conflict about AJA. Will I ever be able to drop it completely? Maybe not. I don't think Jung ever got over the pain of Freud's unjust treatment of him. And yet I can see that his departure from the psychoanalytic camp was an essential part of his development. Why could he not see it and accept it? The same reason that I find it difficult to forgive AJA. Self made it happen, but ego is still suffering the pain of it. I should love to be able to forgive and forget. Jules and the rest of the group are now fully fledged analysts and have finished the training. Again, my ego is envious—even though I don't need the qualification or the acknowledgement. I would not want to belong to AJA, even if they asked me. It is my complex about being excluded that minds. Another thing I sense in myself, as I talked with Jules, was a sibling rivalry and great feelings of inferiority. She is such a clever, intelligent, and well-educated girl. I feel mealy-mouthed and pedestrian by comparison. I think she would be very surprised if I told her that's how she makes me feel.

MARRIAGE IN PERIL

DURING A HOLIDAY in the United States in 1982, I started to become aware of the defects in our marriage. I remember sitting on the plane on the journey to JFK airport, pondering why I felt so unhappy, so unattractive, and overweight. I knew that I ate to comfort myself when I was unhappy, but I wondered if being fat was the reason I felt so unattractive. Why couldn't I feel vibrant and sexy as I did when I was with Ury? He didn't care what shape or size I was. As the plane started its descent, I began to see that Francis's attitude to me made me feel lump-like and unattractive. The anima part of me that had come to life through the relationship with Ury, was still very young and unformed. Because Francis didn't recognise it, it had retreated.

Over the next few days, I wondered how I could access the anima part of myself, even if there was no one to constellate it. I told myself that the stage of development I had reached was not unlike what I experienced when Belinda was born. Then I lived to the full with joy and happiness the feelings of being a mother—not copying or reacting against anybody else, but trusting my own feelings—and finding within myself the good mother. I was totally relaxed and confident with Belinda. I did everything my way, responding to her needs and wallowing in the joy of her.

I knew the anima was as vital a part of my personality as the good mother, but I was not very confident about using it. This only could be done in my own way—not copying anybody else or trying too hard, but by relaxing and feeling confident—finding and being that part of myself. With Belinda, I knew the good mother was there and I knew it was right. With anima, I also knew it was there and it was right.

But surely, I asked myself, Francis's inability to see the anima in me couldn't be the reason I was feeling so desperately unhappy? I wondered if going to the States for a month's holiday with the family revived memories of leaving England in 1940 and becoming refugees in Princeton, New Jersey for five years. Then, I had left the security and love of Nanny, who had looked after me since I was born, for the negative projections of my mother. Now I was leaving the love and security of Sasha and Ury for Francis's negative projections.

There were two very separate layers in me. The top layer, the conscious layer, was a girl who tried hard to be good—to be a good wife, mother, employee. I liked being married and the idea of being part of a happy marriage. I didn't dare criticise Francis. Sometimes I got cross with him (and nearly always apologised afterwards) but I didn't stand back and look at him critically. I accepted him at his own valuation; it suited me to do so. I wanted him to be the sort of man he pretended to be—honest, hard-working, reliable, a misunderstood artist who one day would receive the acknowledgement he deserved. I ignored his disloyalty, his discourtesy to me in public, his continual denigration of me, his lack of support or help, and his inability to love. I didn't let myself see any of this. My admiration of my mother had started to crack at the time of Faye's illness, but my relationship with Francis, and my rigid, undeveloped personality, were still encased in an adolescent facade—playing at being a wife and mother, just as Francis played at being a good husband. But cracks in the facade were starting to appear.

A few days before we left for our holiday, I wrote about this in my journal, though I did not recognise at that time how much of the panic of going to the States was fear of being trapped by Francis.

JOURNAL (July 1982) Feelings about going to the States next weekend: I don't want to go. I'm leaving everything behind. Will I come back? Will I survive the month? The same feeling as I had at 5—will it be the same now? Will I lose the peace and contentment I have at the moment and then find I cannot regain it? Maybe then I looked forward to the adventure, as Belinda and Alexander are now, but in reality it was painful, cruel and distressing; that was when paradise disappeared. I thought for ever. Now I have found it again—and the thought of going to the States, repeating that journey, fills me with dread. Francis and the children will be with me—but the pain of the 1940–45 years sometimes overwhelms me—memories of feeling abandoned at camp, left out of games by Juliet, lying in bed sobbing and my mother coming in and asking me what was the matter. Saying, "I'm missing Daddy" because I couldn't tell her my real misery was missing Nanny.

We had exchanged houses with an American family in Upstate New York. Each day we went on outings, returning in the late afternoon when I would cook supper. Tina was not very happy with the holiday because there were no friends for her. Simon, by this time had left home, and did not come with us. Tina rarely talked to me and didn't offer to help with any of the household chores. Here I felt paralysed by Francis's criticisms. If I asked the children to help, he would say, "Leave the children alone. It is your job."

Francis's lack of consideration towards me was highlighted by a trivial event one evening. I was feeling happy and quite amorous towards Francis, until at ten o'clock I went to bed and found, to my dismay, that Tina had taken the cassette player so I couldn't listen to music as I had intended. I went to Francis (Tina had gone to bed) and he said he had told her she could have it. It was an unimportant incident except for the effect it had on me. I felt fed up and cross with Francis for not considering me or even asking me first. I was so put out by it that I couldn't sleep. I realised it was an over-reaction, and, as I lay in bed, I tried to work out why this upset me so much. Listening to music was often the precursor to writing active imaginations. By taking away the cassette player, Francis was blocking me from the most important part of my life. As the night progressed, I became more and more gloomy. I began to see that Francis blocked me in everything that mattered to me. I felt he was a malign influence in my life and the marriage was rotten at its core.

Over the remaining days of the holiday, I pushed aside the negative thoughts that had arisen during those dark hours of the night, and tried to enjoy the time with Francis and the children. To assuage my unhappiness, I wrote copious letters to Ury and each day walked down to the mailbox at the bottom of the drive to see if there was a letter from him, which I wanted to intercept before the family saw it and asked me who it was from. I counted the days until we returned home. Every evening, I did active imaginations; but reading them now I can see they were done to comfort myself, they did not come from the unconscious.

I consulted the *I Ching*:

What is wrong with me, what should I do?
Hexagram 23 (Splitting apart)
"It does not further one to go anywhere."
Hexagram 29 (The Abysmal)
"An individual finds himself in an evil environment to which he is committed by external ties. But he has an inner relationship with a superior man and through this he retains the stability to free

himself from the way of the inferior people around him. This brings
him into opposition with them of course, but that is not wrong."

I went through each day fitting in with the family, going on expeditions, cooking the meals. But I felt I was only existing, not living. I was counting the days to our return home when I could start living again.

I thought a lot about my relationship with Francis. I puzzled about why I felt enclosed, protected and, in a way, stifled. He was very loving, sensitive, super to the children, and appeared to be considerate to me, and yet there was a dark undertow that I was only now becoming conscious of. It had a claustrophobic effect on me. Unlike previous holidays, we did not quarrel and there were only two things that caused our feathers to be ruffled. If I read the newspaper that was fine with Francis, but if I read a book, he made some caustic comment; if I referred to something I was reading, he denigrated it or made a sneering remark. For instance, I said to him one morning that I was reading Lao Tzu and finding it very interesting, that it had been given to me by Penelope, and Francis said, "She would!" which effectively silenced me. He was also very strange about money. He was restrictive and critical of whatever I spent on housekeeping. For instance, when I came out of the supermarket yesterday, having spent $10 on food, he would say, "you don't need all this stuff" and make me feel guilty, and yet when I spent $24 on dungarees for Belinda, he didn't mind at all.

It was as if the scales had fallen from my eyes. I was beginning to perceive the sick dynamic between us. Francis was trying to control me, to hold on to me by undermining my confidence. In the past, I had not been aware of what was happening and would become sulky and bad tempered–then we would have a row–I'd apologise and we would be on an even keel again. Now, I didn't know how to respond to him. I was consumed with anger and vented my feelings in my journal.

JOURNAL Oh God! Oh God! Why did I get myself into this mess? Tie myself up to such a pathetic man! I despise him and I'm so full of pain at the way he treats me. When I see my guilty reactions, it makes me so angry I could weep. He tries to hook me on guilt all the time; until now I have responded. Can it ever change? Is this just one more knot in the marital tangle? Other things have improved. But not enough. I *know* it can change—if he were a patient, I would not feel so gloomy. The pain is, I think, the memories of thirty years of functioning like this.

During the next three years, 1984-6, the marriage was in a perilous condition. It was as if, having left a safe harbour, I was navigating a ship over stormy waters, a ship that was full of holes and liable to sink at any moment. The safe harbour was the marriage as it had been for nearly thirty years. But I knew I could no longer be content in the relationship as it was. At that time, not only was I trying to change our sick interaction, my perception of Francis was also changing.

DREAM Francis is burning in a pyre in the garden—tied to a stake—he is very stoical—it must hurt but he does not cry out. Alexander and I watch him. As fire reaches his head, I nearly call out, "Francis, I love you".

This dream was extremely powerful and still resonates with me today. I remember taking the dream to Adler. He was puzzled by it and did not pursue any of the images in it. If we had worked together on the dream to reveal its meaning, Adler would have learnt that I was not lying when I said I was happily married. My projection of the perfect husband extended to the marriage. A good marriage was essential to me: my parents had been divorced and I was determined that my marriage would succeed.

As I pondered the meaning of this dream over the following months, I came to realise it was telling me that my love for Francis was burning on a pyre like an effigy of Guy Fawkes. It was a projection that I loved, not the real man. It was this projection in the dream that was burning, dissolving and enabling me to see Francis as he really was. From the moment I had met Francis, I had invested him with qualities which did not belong to him. Alexander, in the dream, represented my young animus that was enabling me to think independently. This dream showed I was withdrawing the projection and starting to see Francis as he really was. I began to realise that he was a hollow man, who relied on people's projections, and was irresistibly attracted to people who admired him. This was the basis of his relationship with Elisabeth Skinner.

Elisabeth Skinner met Francis soon after Belinda was born and offered to help him with his concerts. She was an attractive woman, with dark hair and a Viennese accent. From the moment she arrived on the scene, I felt jealous of her. I never felt she was supportive of me, in fact the opposite. She would spend hours with Francis in his studio, which was in the garden, separate from the house. I never had the confidence to remonstrate or stand up to her in any way; in fact, I did not think I had any grounds to do so, until one fateful afternoon. I went over to the studio and found them on the sofa together and Francis was kissing her. I was appalled and told him I never wanted her in the house again. For some time, Francis accepted this, and Elisabeth stopped helping him with the concerts. But when I started at Brunel, she eased her way into his life again, surreptitiously at first, and then more openly.

The prospect of trying to improve our marriage felt overwhelmingly difficult. It seemed an impossible task. How could I help Francis to change when he didn't want to or see the need to? Was the way forward, I wondered, to show him the need? Then I felt scared at my presumption. I always felt uneasy when Ury suggested we should force a patient to see his problems. Were we right to do so? To interfere in somebody's life—make judgements about them? How did we know what was right for somebody else? I felt blocked by Francis, and I was beginning to see why—but was I right to try to change him?

> JOURNAL The most worrying thing in my life is Francis. He is so mixed up and blocked: negative in his reaction to me and unrealistic in his attitude to the world. I am trying to get more honesty and realism into our relationship, to get the negative feelings out into the open, but this causes pain to both of us. I feel hopeless about him. Is he capable of change? Is there any future for our relationship?

Why didn't I walk away from the marriage at this point? Why was I so determined to keep it going? This was because I had invested so much in it: we had four children; our friends and family saw us as a happy couple; I didn't want to follow the route my parents had taken. I wanted my relationship with Francis to improve and I was optimistic that he could change—it would be in his interest to do so—and that we could forge a new relationship together.

As I began to look at the relationship more objectively, I saw that in public situations Francis was often rude and discourteous to me because he knew I couldn't object when other people were there. In these situations I would feel paralysed and I didn't know what to do. Walk out? Confront him? It frequently ended with us sitting in sullen silence.

I also became aware that at home, when we were having supper with Belinda and Alexander (Simon and Tina had now left home) Francis used the children as a shield, and undermined everything I said, implying I was difficult and that anything that went wrong was my fault. He knew I wouldn't remonstrate because I was trapped. I didn't want to upset the children by attacking him; I didn't want them in the crossfire. On these occasions, Alexander tended to copy Francis. Belinda would take my side, wondering what the hell was going on. I was left fuming and miserable.

When we were on our own, Francis could be charming. Then he didn't have other people or the children to protect him. On our own, I was able to talk to him about his behaviour to me, also show him his behaviour in relation to other people. He was subservient to people in authority, such as policemen, but rude to people he thought were his inferiors, such as waiters. He had been so offensive to our doctor that the whole family were thrown off the doctor's list and I had the unenviable task of trying to find another doctor who would take us on. When I tried to show him how he behaved, he appeared to understand what I was saying.

There was another dynamic to our sick interaction that I could now see.

JOURNAL There is an unconscious contract between us—based on his weakness—and I feel as if I am betraying him by showing him up publicly. But in fact, it is only one step further from confronting him in private. In future, if he takes me on in public because he senses that I won't show him up, I will warn him, and if he persists, confront him just as I would if we were alone.

One evening, we went to a lecture together and then on to supper at an Italian restaurant in South Kensington, an effort on both our parts towards reconciliation. While we were having supper, Francis told me there was a rehearsal in the studio the following Wednesday and that the musicians would use the kitchen in the house for their coffee break. This had been a point of dissension between us on many occasions. I knew he was bringing it up now because he thought I wouldn't argue about it in a public place. But this time I wasn't going to conform, and we had an acrimonious argument.

"I am happy for the musicians to use the kitchen but you or Elisabeth must provide the coffee, tea and biscuits for them. I do not want them to use the stuff I've bought for the family," I said.

"What utter nonsense," Francis said. "Of course, the musicians can eat our biscuits. If you're so bothered about it, I'll buy you a packet of biscuits."

Our voices became louder as we argued, and I was aware of people at the other tables looking at us. But I was determined to stand my ground. For years, it had felt wrong to me when musicians used our kitchen and ate the biscuits I had bought for the children. As in all my arguments with Francis, I had to ask myself, what was normal behaviour? If this was happening in somebody else's house, how would they expect the musicians to behave? I told myself that the organisers of the concerts would provide the coffee and biscuits. They would not expect the owner of the house to provide them. And, in addition, they would thank the owner for kindly allowing them to use her kitchen.

It all seemed so trivial, and I felt ungenerous and mean-spirited as I tried to get Francis to see my point of view. The argument was not about biscuits, it was about Francis disregarding my feelings and riding roughshod over me. I could see that he had learnt nothing over the past months—that any improvement had just been cosmetic manoeuvres to keep me happy.

Another point of concern for me was Francis's concerts. His main occupation was running a series of concerts of contemporary British music, for which the Arts Council gave him a grant to partially fund the fees of the performers and hire of the hall. These concerts were held on the South Bank in the Purcell Room. I always supported him by going to his concerts but often felt embarrassed because there were so few people in the audience. Also, it was obvious to me that, contrary to what he thought, Francis was not respected in the musical profession; the musicians who took part in his concerts did so because he was paying them and giving them a platform.

I was in a familiar trap—the trap was between Francis and my mother. Nancy was a staunch supporter of Francis and came to every concert and did everything she could to promote his career. And I did likewise. I was the little wife supporting her husband through thick and thin. Francis often spoke to Nancy on these occasions but never acknowledged me. He never spoke to me or sat with me; in fact he behaved at his concerts as if I didn't exist. I knew that if Francis came to a lecture of mine, I would thank him for coming and introduce him to other people there.

Ury asked me why I was putting up with it. He suggested that my attitude to Francis's concerts was hypocritical. I rarely had occasion to feel proud—mostly had a sinking feeling of misery. Elisabeth Skinner, playing manipulative games, added to my unhappiness. Why did I tolerate it? I explained to Ury that if I said to Francis, "I will not come to any of your concerts until you treat me as a wife," he would say, "Okay, don't come then."

JOURNAL Last night, I didn't really sleep at all. I realise this is always the case when I am sorting things out—ego starts wobbling and sleep goes up the spout. I am beginning to wonder if taking sleeping pills is the wrong strategy. It is mucking about with my body—manipulating it. Psyche is saying to me, "Sort this out." I am saying to it, "Go to sleep". Arrogant and wrong. But I feel scared at the prospect of night after night of no sleep.

After mulling it over for most of the night, I decided that I would not go to another concert of Francis's until he asked me to come and valued my presence. What would I be missing? There had been precious little of note in the hundreds of concerts I had attended, so I would be missing very little. My anxiety was about changing a pattern of behaviour that had existed all our married life.

I asked the *I Ching:*

What should I do about my marriage?

Hexagram 39 (Obstruction)

"Difficulties and obstructions throw a man back upon himself.
While the inferior man seeks to put the blame on other persons,
bewailing his fate, the superior man seeks the error within himself,
and through this introspection the external obstacle becomes for
him an occasion of inner enrichment and education."

In July 1984, Tina married Ben Green, a fellow medical student. We held the reception at our house in Chiswick.

JOURNAL I think I got it right at Tina's wedding—an afternoon when I felt tranquil and centred—very unusual for me at a large event. There I was being myself and opening my house to all these people, showing them my family and children. I wasn't really concerned with their opinion of me/us. I knew what I was offering was lovely and good—I knew some people would bitch—others would love it—and I was just happy and grateful to be in that position. If I had taken the line—this is the most important wedding or I have something special to offer—it would have clashed—as Francis's pompous speech did.

As the summer holidays approached, I realised that I had to work on my part in the relationship so that we could enjoy the summer together. Foremost, I needed to take control of the holiday arrangements. Practical things are a problem for me, and I tended to let Francis take charge so that I didn't have to worry about them. I realised I needed to step up and do it myself. It was not good for me or for our marriage for me to opt out of using my inferior function, sensation. I knew it was laziness and cowardice on my part to leave all the arrangements—booking the hotels, arranging car hire, sorting out currency—to Francis. I began to realise that leaving the organising to Francis didn't help me, because he never told me what he was doing and I would become increasingly anxious as the holiday approached, wondering if he had made any arrangements at all. In this way, I allowed him to control and dominate me.

Money became a point of contention between us as I tried to make our relationship more honest and real. Contrary to what everybody thought, Francis did not support the family financially. My earnings plus the family trust funds were the source of all our income. Francis had convinced himself that the money was his, and he had full control of it. I realised that I had contributed to Francis's strange attitude. For twenty-eight years, I had colluded in his fantasy that the money was his. It was a fantasy I had perpetuated, because of my fear that the money would destroy his potency in relation to me. I wanted him to feel that he was head of the family—I didn't want my family's money to emasculate him, as had happened to my father. When Francis and I married, I gave him control of my money. Looking back, I can see it was naive to do so, but it was not unreasonable to want Francis to feel good about his position in the family. What was unreasonable was that he abused his position to the point where he contributed nothing to the family expenses and pretended to himself and others that my money was his.

JOURNAL Francis has such a strange attitude to money. Everything I have is his. But everything he has is his—and I'm like a vampire in even asking what he has. He has repressed all feelings of guilt/embarrassment in relation to my family's money—and looks upon it as his. I think I'm getting through to him that it isn't—and that he should contribute to the family expenses too.

The main argument, which we returned to over and over again, was about the joint account, out of which Francis paid the family bills. All the money in the joint account came from me. When I pointed this out to him, he said I was being selfish and grasping, that it was joint money, as much his as mine. Then I realised I had to take a decisive step. I opened a new bank account and stopped payments into the joint account and arranged that in future all the bills should be sent to me. Taking control of the money was more frightening than standing up to Francis. I was frightened of money; I didn't really understand it and I didn't know how to handle it. I had always let other people look after my money. I realised that I needed to face this fear. Quite apart from the problems with Francis, I needed to take control of my own money. Although I knew this would be scary, I was determined to do it. By facing my fear of practical things, I was moving forward in my individuation.

As the months progressed, I tried to hold onto my belief that Francis could change, that we could achieve a happy relationship together. But slowly it dawned on me that Francis was an unpleasant and selfish man who was never going to change. There were things I still liked about him—his intelligence, his sense of humour, his love for the children, but all the rest was repulsive and I felt defeated by it. I was no longer prepared to put up with his bullying and negative attitude. The last straw was when he refused to admit that he had been reading my journal.

JOURNAL (April 1986) With sorrow, I realise Francis has been searching for this journal and has read it. It makes me despise him and feel considerable sorrow. Despise—because he does not admit this is what he has done. Sorrow—because of the pain it will cause him. He can never understand what Ury and I were about, not unless he has the courage to openly admit why he knows I am "running about with other men," as he calls it. He looks down on me and, as ever, imputes all the most negative qualities to what I do.

How can I cope with this? I feel despairing—because what sort of marriage is this? How can we ever be happy together? I understand his anxiety and insecurity. In his shoes, I would feel the same. But if he had respected my privacy, this would not have happened. But, as it stands, he has got himself into the position where he will not admit that he has read the journal. If he did, could I explain? Yes, I think so—if there was respect on both sides.

But there is no respect. He despises me—he treats me as a bad woman. He understands nothing and does not want to. So I feel tonight that our marriage is over. I never wanted this to happen; there was no need for it. I realise that our marriage ending is a singular failure.

I handled the end of the marriage very badly. I hadn't prepared anybody for it because I hadn't shared with anybody my difficulties with Francis and my struggles to keep the marriage intact. Therefore, my family and friends were appalled and shocked. The only person who would have been pleased was my father, but by that time he had died. My sister burst into tears when I told her. My mother immediately supported Francis and suggested marriage counselling. Francis went round telling everybody that I was having a breakdown, which caused me great embarrassment. When I went to see the doctor about some minor ailment, he asked me if I was hearing voices. At the children's school, on parents' evening, the teachers were reluctant to talk to me and looked at me in a very strange way.

Simon was the only one who took the news with equanimity. "Much better to end it if it's not working," he said. There was nobody to talk to about my problems. My relationship with Ury was fading and he was very scared about being implicated in a divorce. I had no close friends at that time in whom I could confide.

It was many years before I recovered my equilibrium. This was compounded by my anguish over Alexander. He was 14 at the time of the divorce and had always taken Francis's side in any argument. He blamed me for breaking up the marriage and thought Francis was an innocent victim. When Francis moved out to live in a house nearby (bought by my family trust) Alexander went to live with him. This broke my heart, not only because I loved him and wanted him with me and Belinda, with whom he had always had a close relationship, but also because I worried about his welfare. He was a very clever boy but also very anxious and immature. I knew Francis would drip poison about me into him and that this would be very harmful to his development. I had always protected the children from the problems in the marriage. I never criticised Francis to them because, in my view, parents are major planks in a child's personality; it is essential that a child feels secure with both.

In retrospect, I think I was wrong in never discussing with the children the difficulties I was facing, because when the marriage ended, it came as a major shock to all of them, except Belinda. Belinda was a very different personality to Alexander. She had a maturity far beyond her age and was very acute in her summing up of people. When she was 15, after Francis had made some caustic remark to me, she said "Mum, why are you putting up with this?" This question of hers was one of the factors that made me take the huge step of going to see a solicitor and filing for divorce.

WILDERNESS

A YEAR AFTER the marriage with Francis ended, Belinda went to university. All the children had now left home, as Alexander was living with Francis. The house seemed huge and very empty. I didn't know what to do with myself. I hated living on my own. I hated going to the supermarket and having only three or four items in a small basket instead of a full trolley. I had no support from friends and family. I couldn't see the way forward. I remember shouting at the sky, "What do you want me to do?" But no answer came. There was a huge void in my life.

My dreams dried up and I was left to my own devices. Why did this happen? Did I cut myself off from the golden string by looking for another husband? At that time, I thought the answer to the emptiness in my life was to marry again. I joined an agency and met a series of unsatisfactory men. And then I met Charles. The fact that he was a retired clergyman attracted me. There was a longing in my heart for fulfilment and I clung on to the memory of those experiences of the numinous. I hoped that joining up with Charles would take me back to the centre, to the Self. But it didn't.

I am usually a good judge of character, but I misread Charles from the beginning. This was partly because I was longing to find a partner; therefore, I discounted my uncertainty about him. It was also because Charles gave a false impression of himself, though not intentionally. All his life he had tried to be what other people wanted him to be. He had been to private school and Oxford, and in both places had struggled to survive. He became a clergyman to please his parents and again he had been out of his depth. Charles was a simple man. He would have been much happier if he had been a gardener. This is where his real interest lay; he knew a lot about plants—growing orchids was his hobby.

I remember, when I was trying to decide whether to marry Charles, I was full of doubt about it. I wrote reams in my journal, columns with reasons for marrying him and columns with reasons against. All the time, I was asking, "What do YOU want me to do" But no answer came. I was adrift and very lonely. Marriage to Charles seemed a good way to proceed.

Quite soon after we married, I was dismayed to find that Charles had little spiritual awareness. He was a clergyman because his father had been, he was a Christian because that is how he grew up. He had never struggled with his faith. He had never questioned anything. He said matins every day and went to church every Sunday because that is what he had always done. I bought a book of religious readings for us to read together, hoping to be able to share with him my thoughts about spirituality. But soon I realised that Charles was not capable of thinking or discussing issues. He was a kind and caring man, but he was not clever and was blinkered in his view of the world.

During the seventeen years of marriage to Charles, the Self faded more and more from my life. I wondered occasionally, "What was all that about?" We bought a sixteenth century house in a village in Kent and created a beautiful garden. This was our main achievement. During this time, Belinda married Graham, and had four children. Visits to Belinda and the children at their house in Cambridge became the most important events in my life. It was as if all the goodness in my life was invested in theirs.

After we moved to Kent, I had intended to continue my private practice and my work at Ashford Hospital, but I started to lose my enthusiasm for the work. I would feel weary when a new patient was referred to me; it was as if I was burnt out and needed a break. Psychology was my passion and yet somehow my feeling about it had dried up. Therefore I resigned from my job at Ashford Hospital and gave up my private practice.

I thought I would get another job in a hospital in Kent. And so I nearly did, except I completely messed up the interview by talking about Adler and my problems with the AJA training scheme. After the interview, I felt devastated. I walked round the orchard opposite our house, asking myself why I had thrown away the job. Did I not want to continue being a psychotherapist? Looking back now, I can see that ego desperately wanted to continue helping other people with their problems; that was what I was good at, and it gave me great satisfaction. Self had other ideas. Being involved in other peoples' lives was a substitute for living my own life. Self wanted me to learn how to live an ordinary life and to be an ordinary person.

I was not very good at it. Everything I tried to do either did not work out or only worked in an incomplete way. I never found real friends in the village, and I never found work that was satisfying. I joined lots of organisations, I became chairman of a local charity, I joined the choir and the committee of the music society and the local walking group. We opened our garden to the public every year. We had a large dog which I walked every day. I was busy, there was lots to do, but nothing was satisfying. I no longer had a sense of purpose or direction.

Now I wonder whether those years with Charles were a necessary exile. *The Hymn of the Robe of Glory*, an eleventh century Gnostic poem, describes such an exile. A young prince is tasked with finding a pearl at the bottom of the sea, guarded by a serpent. The young man ventures into Egypt, wearing "thy robe and thy mantle that goeth upon it." The way was hard and dangerous. He meets up with other young men, forgets his task and forgets that he is a king's son. "I forgot all concerning the pearl for which my parents had sent me." His parents become anxious and send him a letter saying, "Remember that glorious robe, thy splendid mantel remember." The young man comes to his senses, finds his royal robe, and brings the pearl from the bottom of the sea back to his parents.

In the poem, the young prince is exiled because he takes the wrong path—he joins up with young men who divert him from his task. Did I take the wrong path? Did I join up with people who diverted me?

During those years with Charles, I don't remember dreaming at all. I'm not even sure that I kept a dream book. Sometimes I would look at the pile of notebooks in corner of my study and wonder what it was all about. I knew the notebooks recorded an extraordinary few years in my life, but I couldn't see the relevance of Jung's discoveries; the collective unconscious, animus, all the concepts that used to excite me, seemed unimportant and uninteresting. But I knew that Jung was still a crucial part of my life.

JOURNAL (January 1998) Obsession isn't the right word for it, but how do you describe this absorbing passion? (Even that is the wrong word). Ever since I started to read Jung—sitting in bed in 1973 or thereabouts, when I had flu—he has been my inspiration. Yes, inspiration is a much better word. Everything that has happened since then has been inspired by his example. He put me in touch with psyche. He showed me how to work with the unconscious. He led me towards the path of individuation. There was a time when I was obsessed by him—Ury must have been irritated by my continual references to Jung—but in recent years I hardly mention him and have not read him for a long time. But he is there—not in the background—more in the foundation of my life.

His name is debased.
If I mention him,
There is a glazed look
A switching off
A lack of interest.

Is it just fashion that causes this reaction?
A concerted effort
To devalue his
Contribution
To erase his work.

Strange that the opposition
Should have been so effective
He was his own worst advocate
His writing obtuse, woolly,
Imprecise.

But his discoveries
Are world-shaking
His courage phenomenal
His inspiration infectious.
It does not matter
That his name is shunned.
His discoveries about human beings
Have charted the way
To transformation.

In re-reading the journals, I came across two letters, both written by me to me in 2001. They cast a light on those strange years with Charles.

Dear V,

You consider yourself high minded, principled, and that there is a 'golden thread' in your life. But, honestly, if you stand back and look at yourself squarely, as I am now doing, what I see is a self-indulgent, selfish woman. What have you done with your life? All that struggle, all those years of anguish and misery, where has it led? To a respectable 60-year-old woman who lives a life of luxury and self-indulgence. Is that really what it was all about? Do you think that your life will have made a penny worth of difference to the world? You have so many advantages—financial security, health, intelligence, education, but you are not using them for the advantage of anybody but yourself. I know that for years you did give your life up to helping other people, but how much did you really help people then and don't you think your motivation was more about helping yourself?

Dear V,

There is a lot of truth in what you say, but I think the situation is more complicated than you perceive. To start with the last point first: all those years of listening to people's problems, immersing myself in their lives, to the exclusion of my family, friends, and my own needs, was, as you rightly say, with mixed motives. I needed to sort myself out and it was partly through my work with patients that I was able to achieve this.

It was not a conscious decision on my part. I didn't think, "I need to work on this, therefore I will go and work in psychiatry where there are lots of crazy people and I will learn that way." As with all the major decisions of my life, my heart led the way. It was only years later that my head was able to understand it. I knew from the moment I started to do counselling that this was the way I wanted to go. I remember when I was a student at the psychiatric hospital, sitting in a ward round, just listening and learning, I would feel a bursting in my heart, a desperate longing to help the patients who were being discussed and a conviction that I would be able to do so.

I too have wondered about those years of anguish. The journals and notebooks are piled in the corner of my study. I read bits of them and wonder what to do with them. They tell an extraordinary story, but until I understand what it was all about, I am unable to tell it. In one sense, I know what it was about. It was an experience of individuation, of the transformation of the personality such as Jung describes; my dreams, active imaginations, journals from that time, record the experience. As I am drawn back, time after time, to those dusty notebooks, some with moth-eaten pages, I wonder what to do with them. Nobody could understand them and decipher the story they tell unless I put it all together. It is my story and only I can tell it. But how? How to do it? That is the conundrum.

There have been two occasions over the past year when that old feeling of emotional turmoil has surfaced. The first took me by surprise and left me nonplussed. I was at a writing workshop, when the tutor asked us to follow an image of a woman in the kitchen. I picked up my pen and my heart started to burst. I was paralysed and unable to write. Was it the image that caused this and if so why this reaction? I was unable to work it out. All I knew was that the emotional turmoil lasted for the rest of the day. It faded as a painful memory of an unexplained reaction. When I went to the first class of the summer term's creative writing course last week, I was amazed to find myself becoming emotional, tearful, churned up to the extent that I made an absolute mess of playing bridge in the afternoon. So, in answer to your question, "What was that all about?" The answer is, "I don't know but writing seems to be the way my heart is leading me."

I have now reached a time in my life which is pleasant, peaceful, and contented. Like you, I sometimes wonder, "What was it all about?" Is this all that I'm meant to do with my life, to cultivate my garden, enjoy my grandchildren, play bridge, read books, do a bit to help people in the village? It feels right; at the moment, there is no restlessness or discontent within me and so this is how I spend my life. But I know that if, tomorrow, I suddenly had a burning conviction that I had to give up everything and go to Africa or become a nun, I would do so.

My heart has always led the way for me—it's a strange burning feeling in my chest, a surging of tears in my throat, an emotional upheaval which often keeps me awake at night. It is this that leads me into new territories. If I don't feel this, I stay as I am. And that is why for these past seventeen years I have led a relatively uneventful and uncreative life. My heart has not said "move on". My heart has been contented.

Although I say in this letter that my heart was contented, I knew my marriage was sterile and boring. I wasn't complaining about it—this was how life was. Everything I did to make life enjoyable, I had to do on my own. I joined a bridge club and played bridge twice a week. I sang in the choir. I travelled all over the world—to South America, to India, and to far flung places such as Bhutan and Nagaland. I joined a London club and went to concerts and theatres in London. Charles did not want to come with me, he did not want to leave home. Although only six years older than me, he was an old man. His favourite occupations were gardening and watching cricket on the television.

It seems to me now that those years were necessary. I had to develop the neglected parts of my personality. The dream of the tower, that I took to Andrea Dykes at the end of my time with AJA, addresses this problem. The unconscious, symbolised by the tower and associated with Jung (Jung's house in Bollingen was called the Tower) is too large in relation to my conscious functioning. As it says in the dream, the house (my personality) could be nice, but it needed to be worked on. I could not be a useful vessel for the incarnation until I had become fully formed. I had to learn how to be an ordinary woman. I had met Francis when I was 19, just emerging from childhood into adulthood. The following thirty-two years were dominated by him. What did I learn during that time with Charles? Nothing about relationships. Charles was a loner. He was kind to me, but we were not close. During those seventeen years, I learnt about committees, intrigues, politics, village hierarchies, how to travel on my own—all the things people have to learn if they are to achieve maturity. I was not very good at it; I made lots of mistakes and achieved very little, but I suspect that was what it was all about.

⚜

Was it for this
All those years of struggle?
The only reminder
A pile of dusty notebooks
Written to relieve the pain,
To record the process.

Was it for this
(Herbaceous borders, dogs, grandchildren, friends)
The urgent movement towards the Self?
Or has the way been lost
By taking the easy route?

Evenings on the sofa,
Hot chocolate, dogs snoring,
Light flickering on the ceiling.
Has serenity displaced the urge to move on?
Only in writing
The gut-wrenching discord returns.
Not vivid, sleep depriving as before,
But glimmers of anguish beckon beneath the surface.

Scratch the clouded pane
By pen on paper
Then there is a faint glow,
An aching familiarity,
An intimacy, a possibility
Of moving on.

ALAN

IN APRIL 2007, I went to a concert at the Queen Elizabeth Hall in London and there I met Alan. I was 72. I wasn't consciously looking for another man, but now I realise I had been searching for him for years. From the moment I met Alan, I knew I had met my soulmate. I was lonely and bored in the relationship with Charles, but there was no reason to leave him—he was never unkind to me and was basically a good man. I would never have left Charles if I hadn't met Alan.

I had seen Alan before at the Vinehall chamber music concerts in Sussex, but I had never spoken to him, and I didn't know his name. At the concerts, I sat at the back of the hall; Alan and his wife, Meg, always sat near the front. I used to watch them, as I did other people in the audience. I admired his kindness to her because she was very disabled. She was a beautiful woman and always dressed elegantly, and he was very attentive to her. It was clear to me that she had Alzheimer's disease. She obviously enjoyed the concerts and listened to the music intently, until one very sad occasion when she began to shout in the middle of a Mozart quartet and Alan had to take her out. Meg never came to the concerts again.

Alan came on his own, looking rather thin and tired. I still didn't know his name.

At the Queen Elizabeth Hall, I saw the nice man from Sussex sitting two rows in front of me. In the interval, I went up to him and said, "What are you doing here?" He seemed delighted to see me and asked me to have a drink with him. I was astounded. I wasn't used to men asking me to have a drink with them and I was overwhelmed by Alan's smile. At that moment, it was as if the world had suddenly become vibrant and alive again. After the concert, Alan took me to an unusual pub near the hall, and then came with me to Waterloo Station to see me onto the train back to Kent.

"I can't believe it. I can't believe it," I muttered to myself over and over again, all the way home on the train, and for days afterwards. It was not just meeting Alan which was so miraculous. It seemed that from that moment the barriers had fallen away, and my purgatory was over. I was again in touch with my inner voice. It was like the fairy story of Sleeping Beauty. With the prince's kiss, I had woken from 100 years of sleep. Later Alan told me that when we met, he was concerned that I would notice that he hadn't shaved. I in turn was concerned he would notice I was wearing hearing aids!

I moved in with Alan within a few weeks. I knew this is where I should be. I wanted to be with Alan, and I wanted to help him look after Meg. I learnt that Alan had met Meg when they were students at Guy's Hospital. He was devoted to her. They never had any children. Meg was diagnosed with Alzheimer's disease when she was 59. Now, eleven years later, she was in the final stages of the disease. She was incontinent, couldn't feed herself, and was unable to speak. Alan had given up his work as an orthodontist and had looked after her devotedly for more than a decade.

Leaving Charles was not traumatic for him or for me. He was sorry to see me go, and his feelings were hurt for a short time, but he was happy living on his own and had several friends in the village. It was less easy for my children. Here was Mum ending another marriage. But as they got to know Alan and saw how happy I was with him, they began to understand what was going on. Alan loved my children and grandchildren and always said how delighted he was to have a ready-made family.

The relationship with Alan was a revelation to me: for the first time in my life, I was experiencing being loved with an amazing, encompassing love, which, in spite of all the difficulties he and I had to face, sustained me and continues to do so. Alan had this extraordinary capacity for love.

At the beginning I knew nothing about him. At the Vinehall concerts, he always arrived in a battered old Jeep. For our first date, when he came to fetch me from my London club where I was staying for the night, I was amazed when he turned up in a very sleek Jaguar. I was also amazed to discover that he had a charming little house in Marylebone, as well as a house in Sussex. His house in Sussex, Pattendens, a large estate of 110 acres, was an idyllic place.

Alan came from a working class family. He had been a scholarship boy at Christ's Hospital school and also had a scholarship to Guy's Hospital where he trained as a dentist. He told me he learnt to speak "proper" English without a suburban accent when he met Meg's family, who disapproved of his humble origins.

Alan had a very successful orthodontic practice in Harley Street. He had also worked for the Sultan of Brunei who paid him incredible fees to go once a month to attend to the royal children.

Our first years together were not at all easy. Both of us had quick tempers and we often exploded at each other, but we quickly made up. Alan was very good at talking about feelings, and also at picking up how I was feeling. But it was not easy at the beginning because we had many problems to solve, predominantly relating to Meg. Compared to many Alzheimer's patients, she was very easy, because she had always been looked after at home with love by Alan. However, she sometimes became frustrated and would knock everything from the table onto the floor; sometimes she would hit me; one time she bit me. But the main difficulty was the sheer physical strain of looking after her. When we had settled her in bed at night, she would stay put until we got her up in the morning, but we couldn't leave her alone during the day. Alan and I shared her care, but it was very tiring, mealtimes in particularly were tedious as it took ages to feed her. Trying to get her up the stairs to go to bed at the end of the day was exhausting. She was taller than me, and sometimes she would go on strike and refuse to move, and there was nothing I could do to shift her.

Some of the problems Alan and I had in those early years were just the problems of two 70-year-old people getting used to living together. He had a very different rhythm of life to me. He liked to lie in bed in the morning until maybe twelve o'clock, and anything that needed to be done, he was very happy to put off to the next day. He was a master of procrastination. I am an early riser, I like to get things done in the morning, I have learnt over the years not to put things off, and always have a to-do list which I work through. Our different rhythms caused us to argue. And at night, when it was about eleven o'clock, I wanted to go to bed, but Alan was happy to continue watching TV.

I remember one row; it was late at night and probably I was overtired. I was so infuriated by Alan that I said, "I'm leaving." I took down a suitcase from the cupboard and started to throw things into it. I had no plan about where to go, I just wanted to get away. But when I tried to open the front door, I found to my fury that Alan had locked it and hidden the key. He insisted that I sit down and tell him why I was so upset. And then he hugged me and told me how much he loved me—so of course I relented, took off my coat and stayed. I had never before been in a relationship like this with somebody who loved me and who cared about my feelings.

Alan was the first person in my life to accept me as I am. With him, I didn't have to edit what I said before I said it, as I did with everybody else. I didn't have to hold back my opinions about anything (even politics on which we disagreed). He had this extraordinarily uncritical and loving attitude. He loved me and he admired me. For me, it was a very healing experience to be accepted as I am, to be free and uninhibited, to feel safe to say whatever I wanted without fear of being criticised or causing offence.

Meg started to deteriorate in July 2008. She remained healthy and fit but she stopped eating and drinking. The doctor referred her to the local hospice. She died three days later. Alan was very upset and, strangely, so was I. I had longed for her to die, I had longed for Alan and me to be on our own together, but when it happened, I felt very sad. I had come to love her; she had felt to me like our handicapped child, and after she died I missed her very much. There was a service for her at the crematorium, where many of Alan's friends attended. He asked me to read at the service Meg's favourite poem, *Snake* by D.H. Lawrence.

Without the responsibility of looking after Meg, we were at last able to have a happy time together. We went on a safari in Kenya to watch game, which thrilled Alan; he was always fascinated by animals. In London we started to live a very sophisticated, glamorous life. Alan loved dressing up for occasions, white tie and tails for the Apothecaries and Mansion House, black tie for his dental fraternity and dinners at his club, the Atheneum. I loved dressing up too and enjoyed this rather grand lifestyle, going to Covent Garden and Glyndebourne, and rolling around the countryside in his luxurious Jaguar. When we were not living the high life, we were at Pattendens, enjoying the peace and seclusion, with walks in the woods with the dogs, peaceful evenings reading books beside the fire. Alan was a good cook and we used to take it in turns to cook meals. He was very welcoming to my family. Although he had no children of his own, he loved children. In fact, his orthodontic practice was predominantly teenage children. He loved my grandchildren and never seemed to mind the house being in chaos when they visited.

Alan taught me about togetherness and how to be in a loving relationship. We did everything together—concerts, theatre, travelling abroad, music festivals, dinners at his club, visiting the children. It was wonderful to experience together with Alan ordinary activities, such as walking the dogs, cooking and shopping. Alan's dog was a brown Labrador called Snowy, who was loving but very unruly. Alan had no idea about discipline, he loved cuddling his dogs and indulging them. My dog, Juno, a golden retriever, joined us after a few months. The dogs would come with us, sitting on the back seat of the Jaguar, when we travelled between Sussex and London. I loved the fact that Alan wanted to do everything with me, he didn't want me to do things on my own. But this also caused friction. "Let's take the dogs for a walk," I'd say on a sunny Sunday afternoon and Alan would reply, invariably, "Not now. In an hour or so."

I first realised that Alan had Alzheimer's when we were on a skiing holiday with the children in Switzerland in 2014. He was lying in bed because he wasn't feeling well. I went in to talk to him, and I sensed an imperceptible change in him; he was no longer in tune with me, he didn't know how I was feeling. The extraordinary closeness we had had was no longer there. He was still Alan, he was still a kind, loving man, but he had lost his unusual gift of sensitivity to other people's feelings. I felt absolutely bereft. I couldn't bear the thought of losing what we had had.

When our doctor agreed with me that Alan had the beginnings of Alzheimer's, it seemed incredibly cruel that both Alan and Meg should suffer from the same disease. I knew the only way I could cope with this crushing blow was to take some sort of action. The alternative was to sink into self-pity and that I wanted to avoid at all costs. I tried to work out a way to ameliorate the situation. I knew the course the disease would take, I knew the toll on the carer. The only way forward that I could see was to join a clinical trial. I thought this could be interesting, and also we would meet other people in the same boat and I would get some support.

I contacted a company in London that specialised in clinical trials and once a month we went there to be seen by a clinical psychologist. I say 'we' because both Alan and I were assessed each month, he for his symptoms and me as his carer. Looking back, I don't think it helped us very much. The monthly interviews were structured to a checklist. There was no opportunity to discuss feelings, or problems, or meet other patients. The Merck drug that was tested on Alan was not successful and was withdrawn after a year. But I am glad that we joined the clinical trial. For a year or so, it gave us both a slim hope that there might be a cure around the corner.

Alzheimer's disease progresses slowly; some things Alan could do, some things he couldn't. He still enjoyed going to events, to opera and concerts, and to seeing his friends at the dental fraternity, but he couldn't cope with his computer anymore and so I took on all our admin. And that is when I began to see that Alan was being defrauded over a property development. After more than a year of lawyers' intervention, the matter was eventually resolved, but it hung over us for several years, and was not resolved completely until after Alan's death.

The last three years of Alan's life were sad and painful. He was no longer the Alan I knew; he was a sweet old man to whom I was devoted, and for whom I was the main carer. A lot of that time is shrouded in a mist of sadness. He had to go into hospital at one point, he was diagnosed with cancer, they recommended radiotherapy, but I didn't pursue this because being in hospital had upset him so much and there didn't seem any point in trying to prolong his life. The last summer at Pattendens was peaceful and sometimes happy. He loved chats with our gardener and enjoyed our new kitten. He tolerated the carers who came so that I could have some time off but would have preferred me to be with him all the time. About two weeks before he died, he started to complain about pain. The district nurse was visiting twice a week, but she couldn't advise about pain relief. I went to see the doctor and he give me medication for Alan which I think was morphine. It may have relieved the pain, but it made Alan paranoid and difficult, not at all like his usual self.

The night he died, he was very restless and unhappy. It was difficult to persuade him to go upstairs to bed. I remember, when eventually he was in bed, he curled up like a young child as I tucked in his covers. I kissed him and said, "You know I love you and you know you love me." He nodded his head. That is the last time I saw him alive. We were sleeping in separate rooms because if I was with him, I worried about him all night. When I came into his bedroom in the morning at about 6:30 a.m., I found him in the bathroom, slumped over the bath, dead. He was cold and stiff, and I couldn't move him. I rang Belinda and Graham to ask what I should do. They advised me to ring 999 to report his death. Three hours later, Belinda arrived, having driven immediately from Oxford. She stayed with me over the next week.

The following weeks passed in a daze. I was extremely fortunate to find an unusual funeral service at Cranbrook, a nearby village. The funeral service was called Holly's. It was unusual in that they told me I could choose whatever type of funeral I wanted and they said, if I wished, I could help them prepare Alan's body for cremation. I went along to Holly's office, an inconspicuous couple of rooms on an industrial estate, and I took with me Alan's favourite outfit—pink trousers and an old blue jumper, which he always wore at Pattendens.

Holly, a charming sensitive woman of about 40, took me into the room where Alan's body lay. Together, we gently and lovingly washed his body and covered it with a sweet smelling oil. As we did so, Holly asked me about Alan, and I described to her what he was like and how much I loved him. Washing his body, covering his body with oil, and then dressing him in his old clothes was a wonderfully healing experience. It was an opportunity to say goodbye to him and to thank him for the years of happiness together. Then Holly told me I could decide what I wanted to happen. I knew I didn't want a formal service in the crematorium—this was not Alan's style. I wanted the emphasis to be on the scattering of his ashes not on the cremation. I told Holly that the cremation should take place without anybody present and that Alan's ashes be placed in a wicker basket which I would collect from her office.

We invited family, friends, and neighbours for the scattering of Alan's ashes. In the woods surrounding Pattendens is a pet cemetery, where Alan and Meg's cats and dogs are buried. In his will, Alan asked for his ashes to be scattered here. A local florist decorated the pet cemetery and it looked beautiful with garlands of white flowers hanging from the trees. During the scattering, my youngest grandson Milo stood very seriously holding the wicker basket containing the ashes. His older brother, George, took a video on his phone of the proceedings. I spoke briefly about Alan and then many other people spoke, spontaneously and unprepared, with their memories of him. At the end, Milo handed me the wicker basket and I scattered the ashes over the pets' graves.

SUMMING UP

THEY SEEM DISTANT, those days so long ago recorded in the journals. But the feelings of tranquillity, happiness, serenity that I have now—I know these are the fruits of those years of turmoil. Only now, in my old age, can I begin to see what it was all about. It seems to make sense now, to fit into a pattern. I am not the same person as I was then, now that the pieces have come together. I don't feel fragmented, anxious and uncertain. I feel at peace.

During most of those years of marriage to Francis, I did not realise he was abusing me. In the early years of the marriage, I welcomed Francis's control and domination. It felt like a safe harbour. It made me feel secure. Even his denigration of me, his ridicule and putting me down, felt right because his attitude was so similar to what I had experienced with my mother. When psyche pushed me into the relationship with Ury, my eyes started to open. I was able to compare the love Ury gave me with the abuse I received from Francis. The relationship with Ury enabled me to eventually leave the marriage. Although Ury faded from my life, the relationship never ended completely because we were working together in the same psychiatric unit. I saw him daily and was concerned by his white, drawn face. He avoided my eyes. We no longer had lunch together. He knew nothing about what was happening in my life and I knew nothing about what was happening in his. When I left Ashford, I do not remember even saying goodbye to him.

In writing this book I have often felt like an amanuensis. The material was all there—my job was to mould it into a readable form. Writing it has clarified for me what I experienced forty years ago, and it has also provided context. My life now makes sense. To experience individuation, to record it, and then to write about it—this seems to be what my life is about. From that moment in the British Museum in March 2020, when it dawned on me that individuation was the most important thing in my life, there has been pressure on me to work on this book—pressure such as I felt before contacting Sasha, pressure such as propelled me into the relationship with Ury. Over the past two years, I have felt the same pressure to write this book. When, on occasion, I put the book aside, I felt adrift, even depressed. Working on this book has been one of the most affirming, rewarding, and challenging experiences of my life. With one exception: I didn't want to write the chapter Marriage in Peril. I didn't want to re-live those years of unhappiness. I didn't want to have Francis in my head. But I knew I had to do it as it was a relevant part of the story.

The Cloak is an important symbol to me. This became clear as I worked on the book. The active imagination of the Cloak has inspired me to write this book, but like all archetypes, the Cloak has a positive and a negative aspect. The Cloak has urged me to record my experience of individuation, but it has also pulled me towards narcissism. The difference between the positive and negative aspects is subtle. The positive aspect urges me to explain individuation so that other people can be inspired by it. The negative aspect tempts me to show off. Here, ego is saying, "look at me." Why does this matter? Because, when ego points to itself, God leaves the room. I heard this wonderful phrase on the radio the other day. A composer was being asked how he wrote a great melody. His reply was, "I don't. If I try to write a great melody, God leaves the room."

Narcissism is when ego attributes to itself Self-like qualities. As I started on the path of individuation and struggled to understand myself, I saw that narcissism was like bindweed, wrapped around my personality, penetrating every aspect of my life, insidiously, unconsciously, choking its natural development. Pulling it out, getting rid of it so that it didn't continually mess up what I did, was something I was unable to achieve. I didn't recognise it as narcissism for many years. I called it the 'need to be special' complex. It said, "Look at me. I'm special, aren't I marvellous." I wondered whether it was a Jewish trait—I recognised it in my grandmother, and my mother, and in members of my family. I began to make progress when I realised that I had to detach myself from the archetype of the hero, the special one. When I realised this, I began, in my mind, to separate ego from Self.

Jung is making the same point when he says you should not name your virtues. He means you should not focus on your talents—ego should not take credit for what belongs to Self. Ego should be open and receptive to Self's demands. "God has no hands but ours," says St Teresa—but ego should never own Self as part of its functioning. That's a real danger and leads to narcissism.

I find gardening not only a reassuring, down to earth occupation, but a brilliant metaphor for the human condition. Plants need the right conditions to thrive, some never make it, some flower too soon or are destroyed by frost, others grow spindly and pale and never flower. But if there is enough rain and sun and not too much wind, if the soil is right and footballs don't cause damage, a plant will grow proud and triumphant and open its flowers to the pollinating bees. I used to think, when I first had a garden, that there were some super-duper plants and those were the ones I wanted to have. It took me some time to realise that most plants on their own are insignificant. It is the combination of different sizes, shapes, textures, and colours, that make the display. Most of us are insignificant, our lives are unimportant, but each of us has a potential, each of us can flower if the conditions are right, and most of us need to be part of a group to achieve this and contribute to the well-being of others.

I don't think we need to be a Mandela to make a difference to the world. 'Difference' or 'influence' are difficult to quantify or to identify. When I look back on the patients I have worked with, some I think I helped, others I'm not sure if I did. It is not possible to know the effect you have on other people. But I do believe we are all connected to each other, how we live our lives contributes to the overall equilibrium. If we do something courageous, even if nobody knows about it—like picking up a spider you are frightened of or refusing to take part in something dishonest—this contributes to the overall well-being of everybody.

At one of the worst times of my life, when it seemed everybody was misjudging me, when the temptation to scream, behave badly, throw the shit around, seemed irresistible, I walked away and bit my tongue. I thought at the time that to retaliate would be hurting myself and losing my self-respect. I think I was right. By walking away, I was able to hold my head high. And not only did it help me; in some strange way it contributed to the overall well-being. Because we are all connected. What happens to one of us creates ripples which affect others.

Looking back, I can see there was often a disconnect between what I was learning in my inner life and what I was experiencing in my outer life. At the time, they seemed to me two separate worlds. My inner world was the most important part of my life. I longed for the evenings when I could do active imaginations; I treasured my dreams and recognised that they often addressed problems in my outer life, and I tried to act on them. I was obedient to my inner voice. But, nevertheless, there was a split, a hiatus, between inner and outer. At that time I was incapable of incorporating the inner world into my outer life, although I knew this was what psyche was urging me to do.

This disconnect between inner and outer was apparent as I agonised about what to do about Ury, about Sasha, and then about Francis. My dreams and active imaginations were like a precious substratum that ran through my life, known only to me (although occasionally shared with Sasha). They were advising me, I listened to them, but most of the time I was unable to act on them. I knew my psyche was pushing me to leave Sasha, I didn't understand why, though I explained it to myself as "too weak" and "boring". Again, with the Adlers, I could have defended myself in a very different way if there had not been the split in me. I was unable to access unconscious resources when confronted by them. How different our interaction would have been if my active imaginations had been integrated into my conscious functioning.

I am beginning to understand that the ability to combine inner wisdom with outer functioning is Sophia, the fourth function that Toni Wolff describes in her book. If only Sophia, the goddess of wisdom, had been around in those traumatic years! But in those days, I wasn't mature enough to be in touch with her. It seems to me, now, that being in touch with Sophia is not something we can consciously achieve. It is a natural development which occurs when the ego is strong enough to co-operate with the unconscious without being overwhelmed.

Most of what has happened to me in my life can be explained reductively. The visions in 1969 can be attributed to a hormone imbalance caused by myxoedema. Dreams can be seen as an epiphenomenon, a by-product of the brain when the individual is asleep. Active imaginations can be described as compensatory fantasies. Reductive explanations are prevalent today because the dominant paradigm is scientific and rational. "Nothing but" is the prevailing statement of reductive explanations. Ury's extraordinary vision of a royal baby being stripped of its robes describes this beautifully. Reductive explanations see the bare bones of the world stripped of all its meaning and numinosity. When Ury had the vision, he realised that he had stripped the world of all its magic because he had been so disillusioned in childhood by his parents and by the country he was living in; therefore, he subscribed to the prevailing scientific and reductive paradigm.

The tragedy for Ury was that he was not strong enough to resist the pull of the dominant paradigm, although the vision showed him the possibility of living a fuller and more creative life. As Jung points out, if rational and critical thinking dominates, life can become impoverished. The reverse is also true—the more of the unconscious and the more of myth we are capable of making conscious, the more of life we integrate. The Gnostic poem, *The Hymn of the Robe of Glory*, makes the same point. The young prince forgets his royal origin because of the company he keeps. In other words, he is overcome by the prevailing ethos. But a letter from his parents brings him to his senses. "Remember that glorious robe, thy splendid mantle remember."

Evelyn Underhill's book, *Practical Mysticism*, underlines so many of the experiences I have had in my life. This doesn't make me a mystic—but it shows me that I am on the same path. Housework, children, gardening, dogs have all been important ingredients—ways of earthing me and keeping me whole. It is remarkable that Underhill in 1911 related the symbolism of alchemy to mysticism, just as Jung related the symbolism of alchemy to individuation.

This morning, listening to an excerpt from St John's Gospel on the radio, it dawned on me that the life of Jesus Christ—foreshadowed in Old Testament prophecies—follows an archetypal pattern—humble birth, misunderstood, suffering, torn between opposites, death, and then new life. This pattern, this myth, underlies individuation. For all of us, individuation begins in a humble way. It often leads to suffering and being misunderstood. It often involves being torn between opposites. But out of the pain and suffering, the path of individuation leads to new life.

I now see that throughout my life individuation has emerged over and over again, and each time I have had to acknowledge it and take responsibility. At 16 when I became a Christian. At 32, acknowledging the visions and leaving the church. When Faye got ill, wrestling with psyche and acknowledging my own inner voice. Through Ury—giving up my whole conception of myself. Then leaving Sasha and realising the spirit in AJA was corrupt. Finally, committing myself to a relationship with Alan. Now, acknowledging the Cloak and recognising what I do has authenticity and value.

At first, I thought the Cloak was a symbol of individuation and so it may be for somebody else, but for me it is more than that. The Cloak symbolises the task I have been given; it is the driving force that directed me to write about those experiences from forty years ago. It is the Cloak that has urged me to write this book, to show other people how individuation can transform their lives.